shakespeare's
a **midsummer
night's dream**

# shakespeare's a midsummer night's dream

## harold bloom

riverhead books

new york

**THE BERKLEY PUBLISHING GROUP**
**Published by the Penguin Group**
**Penguin Group (USA) Inc.**
**375 Hudson Street, New York, New York 10014, U.S.A.**
Penguin Group (Canada), 10 Alcorn Avenue, Toronto, Ontario, Canada M4V 3B2
(a division of Pearson Penguin Canada Inc.)
Penguin Books Ltd., 80 Strand, London WC2R 0RL, England
Penguin Group Ireland, 25 St. Stephen's Green, Dublin 2, Ireland
(a division of Penguin Books, Ltd.)
Penguin Group (Australia), 250 Camberwell Road, Camberwell, Victoria 3124, Australia
(a division of Pearson Australia Group Pty., Ltd.)
Penguin Books India Pvt. Ltd., 11 Community Centre, Panchsheel Park, New Delhi —
110 017, India
Penguin Group (NZ), Cnr. Airborne and Rosedale Roads, Albany, Auckland, New Zealand
(a division of Pearson New Zealand, Ltd.)
Penguin Books (South Africa) (Pty.) Ltd., 24 Sturdee Avenue, Rosebank, Johannesburg
2196, South Africa

Penguin Books Ltd., Registered Offices: 80 Strand, London, WC2R 0RL, England

PRINTING HISTORY
Riverhead trade paperback edition: October 2004

Library of Congress Cataloging-in-Publication Data

Bloom, Harold.
   Shakespeare's A midsummer night's dream / Harold Bloom.—1st Riverhead trade
pbk. ed.
      p. cm.
   The essay "A midsummer night's dream" was previously published as part of Shakespeare : invention of the human, by Harold Bloom, published by Riverhead in 1998.
   Includes the full text of the play, with editorial revisions by Harold Bloom.
   ISBN 1-59448-009-5
   1. Shakespeare, William, 1564–1616. Midsummer night's dream. 2. Hippolyta (Greek
mythology)—Drama. 3. Theseus (Greek mythology)—Drama. 4. Athens (Greece)—
Drama. 5. Courtship—Drama. I. Shakespeare, William, 1564–1616. Midsummer
night's dream. II. Bloom, Harold. Shakespeare. III. Title.

PR2827.B66 2004
22.3'3—dc28
                                                          2004050847

PRINTED IN THE UNITED STATES OF AMERICA

10  9  8  7  6  5  4  3  2  1

# contents

author's note     vii

harold bloom on
## a midsummer night's dream    1

william shakespeare
## a midsummer night's dream    31
synopsis    33
dramatis personæ    39

The text of *A Midsummer Night's Dream*, including the synopsis, is that of the old Cambridge Edition (1893), as edited by William Aldis Wright. I am grateful to Brett Foster for indispensable advice upon the editorial revisions I have made in the text.

—Harold Bloom

harold bloom on

# a midsummer night's dream

In the midst of the winter of 1595–96, Shakespeare visualized an ideal summer, and he composed *A Midsummer Night's Dream,* probably on commission for a noble marriage, where first it was played. He had written *Richard II* and *Romeo and Juliet* during 1595; just ahead would come *The Merchant of Venice* and Falstaff's advent in *Henry IV, Part One.* Nothing by Shakespeare before *A Midsummer Night's Dream* is its equal, and in some respects nothing by him afterward surpasses it. It is his first undoubted masterwork, without flaw, and one of his dozen or so plays of overwhelming originality and power. Unfortunately, every production of it that I have been able to attend has been a brutal disaster, with the exception of Peter Hall's motion picture of 1968, happily available on videotape. Only *The Tempest* is as much distorted in recent stagings as *A Midsummer Night's Dream* has been and is likely to go on being. The worst I recall are Peter Brook's (1970) and Alvin Epstein's (a Yale hilarity of 1975), but I cannot be the only lover of the play who rejects the prevailing notion that sexual violence and bestiality are at the center of this humane and wise drama.

Sexual politics is too much in fashion for me just to shudder and pass by; *A Midsummer Night's Dream* will reassert itself, at a better time than this, but I have much to say on behalf of Bottom, Shakespeare's most engaging character before Falstaff. Bottom, as the play's text comically makes clear, has considerably less sexual interest in Titania than she does in him, or than many recent critics and directors have in her. Shakespeare, here and elsewhere, is bawdy but not prurient; Bottom is amiably innocent, and not very bawdy. Sex-and-violence exalters really should look else-where; *Titus Andronicus* would be a fine start. If Shakespeare had desired to write an orgiastic ritual, with Bottom as "this Bacchic ass of Saturnalia and carnival" (Jan Kott), we would have a dif-ferent comedy. What we do have is a gentle, mild, good-natured Bottom, who is rather more inclined to the company of the elves—Peaseblossom, Cobweb, Moth, and Mustardseed—than to the madly infatuated Titania. In an age of critical and theatrical absurdity, I may yet live to be told that Bottom's interest in the little folk represents a potential for child abuse, which would be no sillier than the ongoing accounts of *A Midsummer Night's Dream*.

It is a curious link between *The Tempest, Love's Labour's Lost,* and *A Midsummer Night's Dream* that these are the three plays, out of thirty-nine, where Shakespeare does not follow a pri-mary source. Even *The Merry Wives of Windsor,* which has no definite source, takes a clear starting point from Ovid. *The Tem-pest* is essentially plotless, and almost nothing happens in *Love's Labour's Lost,* but Shakespeare uniquely took pains to work out a fairly elaborate and outrageous plot for *A Midsummer Night's Dream*. Inventing plot was not a Shakespearean gift; it was the one dramatic talent that nature had denied him. I think he prided himself on creating and intertwining the four different worlds of character in the *Dream*. Theseus and Hippolyta belong to ancient myth and legend. The lovers—Hermia, Helena, Lysander, and Demetrius—are of no definite time or place, since all young people in love notoriously dwell in a common element. The fairies—Titania, Oberon, Puck, and Bottom's four chums—emerge from literary folklore and its magic. And finally, the "mechanicals" are English rustic artisans—the sublime Bottom, Peter Quince, Flute, Snout, Snug, and Starveling—and so come out of Shakespeare's own countryside, where he grew up.

This mélange is so diverse that a defense of it becomes the hidden reference in the wonderfully absurd exchanges between Theseus and Hippolyta concerning the music of the hounds in Act IV, Scene i, lines 103–27, which I will consider in some detail later. "So musical a discord, such sweet thunder" has been widely and correctly taken as this play's description of itself. Chesterton, who sometimes thought the *Dream* the greatest of all Shakespeare's plays, found its "supreme literary merit" to be "a merit of design."

As an epithalamium, the *Dream* ends with three weddings, and the reconciliation of Oberon and Titania. But we might not know that all this was an extended and elaborate marriage song if the scholars did not tell us, and from the title on we do know that it is (at least in part) a dream. Whose dream? One answer is: Bottom's dream or his weaving, because he *is* the protagonist (and the greatest glory) of the play. Puck's epilogue, however, calls it the audience's dream, and we do not know precisely how to receive Puck's apologia. Bottom is universal enough (like Joyce's Poldy Bloom or Earwicker) to weave a common dream for all of us, except insofar as we are Pucks rather than Bottoms. How are we meant to understand the play's title? C. L. Barber pointed out Dr. Johnson's error in believing that "the rite of May" must take place on May Day, since the young went Maying when the impulse moved them. We are neither at May Day nor at Midsummer Eve, and so the title probably should be read as *any* night at all in midsummer. There is a casual, throwaway gesture in the title: this could be anyone's dream or any night in midsummer, when the world is largest.

Bottom is Shakespeare's Everyman, a true original, a clown rather than a fool or jester. He is a wise clown, though he smilingly denies his palpable wisdom, as if his innocent vanity did not extend to such pretension. One delights in Falstaff (unless one is an academic moralist), but one loves Bottom, though necessarily he is the lesser figure of the two. No one in Shakespeare, not even Hamlet or Rosalind, Iago or Edmund, is more intelligent than Falstaff. Bottom is as shrewd as he is kind, but he is not a wit, and Falstaff is Monarch of Wit. Every exigency finds Bottom round and ready: his response is always admirable. The Puck-induced metamorphosis is a mere externality: the inner Bottom is unfazed and immutable. Shakespeare foregrounds Bottom by showing us that he is the favorite of his fellow mechanicals: they acclaim him as "bully Bottom," and we learn to agree with them.

Like Dogberry after him, Bottom is an ancestor of Sheridan's Mrs. Malaprop, and uses certain words without knowing what they signify. Though he is thus sometimes inaccurate at the circumference, he is always sound at the core, which is what Bottom the Weaver's name means, the center of the skein upon which the weaver's wool is wound. There are folkloric magical associations attendant upon weaving, and Puck's choice of Bottom for enchantment is therefore not as arbitrary as first it seems. Whether or not Bottom (very briefly) becomes the carnal lover of the Fairy Queen Shakespeare leaves ambiguous or elliptical, probably because it is unimportant compared with Bottom's uniqueness in the *Dream:* he alone sees and converses with the fairy folk. The childlike fourfold of Peaseblossom, Moth, Cobweb, and Mustardseed are as charmed by Bottom as he is by them. They recognize themselves in the amiable weaver, and he beholds much that is already his own in them. "On the loftiest of the world's thrones we still are sitting on our own Bottom," Montaigne taught Shakespeare and the rest of us in his greatest essay, "Of Experience." Bottom the natural man is also the transcendental Bottom, who is just as happily at home with Cobweb and Peaseblossom as he is with Snug and Peter Quince. For him there is no musical discord or confusion in the overlapping realms of the *Dream*. It is absurd to condescend to Bottom: he is at once a sublime clown and a great visionary.

## 2

There is no darkness in Bottom, even when he is caught up in an enchanted condition. Puck, his antithesis, is an ambivalent figure, a mischief maker at best, and something weirder also, though the play (and Oberon) confine him to harmlessness, and indeed bring benignity out of his antics. Puck's alternate name in both the play and in popular lore is Robin Goodfellow, more a prankster than a wicked sprite, though to call him "Goodfellow" suggests a need to placate him. The word *puck* or *pook* originally meant a demon out for mischief or a wicked man, and Robin Goodfellow was once a popular name for the Devil. Yet throughout the *Dream* he plays Ariel to Oberon's Prospero, and so is under firmly benign control. At the end of the play, Bottom is restored to his external guise, the lovers pair off sensibly, and Oberon and Titania resume their union. "But we are spirits of another sort," Oberon remarks, and even Puck is therefore benevolent in the *Dream*.

The Puck–Bottom contrast helps define the world of the *Dream*. Bottom, the best sort of natural man, is subject to the pranks of Puck, helpless to avoid them, and unable to escape their influence without Oberon's order of release: though the *Dream* is a romantic comedy, and not an allegory, part of its power is to suggest that Bottom and Puck are invariable components of the human. One of the etymological meanings of "bottom" is the ground or the earth, and perhaps people can be divided into the earthy and the puckish, and are so divided within themselves. And yet Bottom is human, and Puck is not; since he has no human feelings, Puck has no precise human meaning.

Bottom is an early Shakespearean instance of how meaning gets started, rather than merely repeated: as in the greater Falstaff, Shakespearean meaning comes from excess, overflow, florabundance. Bottom's consciousness, unlike Falstaff's and Hamlet's, is not infinite; we learn its circumferences, and some of them are silly. But Bottom is heroically sound in the goodness of his heart, his bravery, his ability to remain himself in any circumstance, his refusal to panic or even be startled. Like Launce and the Bastard Faulconbridge, Bottom is a triumphant early instance of Shakespeare's invention of the human. All of them are on the road to Falstaff, who will surpass them even in their exuberance of being, and vastly is beyond them as a source for meaning. Falstaff, the ultimate anarchist, is as dangerous as he is fascinating, both life-enhancing and potentially destructive. Bottom is a superb comic, and a very good man, as benign as any in Shakespeare.

# 3

Doubtless Shakespeare remembered that in Edmund Spenser's *The Faerie Queene* Oberon was the benevolent father of Gloriana, who in the allegory of Spenser's great epic represented Queen Elizabeth herself. Scholars believe it likely that Elizabeth was present at the initial performance of the *Dream,* where necessarily she would have been the Guest of Honor at the wedding. *A Midsummer Night's*

*Dream,* like *Love's Labour's Lost, The Tempest,* and *Henry VIII,* abounds in pageantry. This aspect of the *Dream* is wonderfully analyzed in C. L. Barber's *Shakespeare's Festive Comedy,* and has little to do with my prime emphasis on the Shakespearean invention of character and personality. As an aristocratic entertainment, the *Dream* bestows relatively little of its energies upon making Theseus and Hippolyta, Oberon and Titania, and the four young lovers lost in the woods into idiosyncratic and distinct personages. Bottom and the uncanny Puck are protagonists, and are portrayed in detail. Everyone else—even the other colorful Mechanicals—are subdued to the emblematic quality that pageantry tends to require. Still, Shakespeare seems to have looked beyond the play's initial occasion to its other function as a work for the public stage, and there are small, sometimes very subtle touches of characterization that transcend the function of an aristocratic epithalamium. Hermia has considerably more personality than Helena, while Lysander and Demetrius are interchangeable, a Shakespearean irony that suggests the arbitrariness of young love, from the perspective of everyone except the lover. But then all love is ironical in the *Dream*: Hippolyta, though apparently resigned, is a captive bride, a partly tamed Amazon, while Oberon and Titania are so accustomed to mutual sexual betrayal that their actual rift has nothing to do with passion but concerns the protocol of just who has charge of a changeling human child, a little boy currently under Titania's care. Though the greatness of the *Dream* begins and ends in Bottom, who makes his first appearance in the play's second scene, and in Puck, who begins Act II, we are not transported by the sublime language unique to this drama until Oberon and Titania first confront each other:

> *Obe.* Ill met by moonlight, proud Titania.
> *Tita.* What, jealous Oberon? Fairies, skip hence; I have forsworn his bed and company.

*Obe.* Tarry, rash wanton; am not I thy lord?
*Tita.* Then I must be thy lady; but I know
    When thou hast stol'n away from fairy land,
    And in the shape of Corin, sat all day
    Playing on pipes of corn, and versing love
    To amorous Phillida. Why art thou here,
    Come from the farthest step of India,
    But that, forsooth, the bouncing Amazon,
    Your buskin'd mistress and your warrior love,
    To Theseus must be wedded, and you come
    To give their bed joy and prosperity?
*Obe.* How canst thou thus, for shame, Titania,
    Glance at my credit with Hippolyta,
    Knowing I know thy love to Theseus?
    Didst not thou lead him through the glimmering night
    From Perigouna, whom he ravished;
    And make him with fair Aegles break his faith,
    With Ariadne and Antiopa?

                               [II.i.60–80]

In Plutarch's *Life of Theseus,* read by Shakespeare in Sir Thomas North's version, Theseus is credited with many "ravishments," cheerfully itemized here by Oberon, who assigns Titania the role of bawd, guiding the Athenian hero to his conquests, herself doubtless included. Though Titania will retort that "These are the forgeries of jealousy," they are just as persuasive as her visions of Oberon "versing love/To amorous Phillida," and enjoying "the bouncing Amazon," Hippolyta. The Theseus of the *Dream* appears to have retired from his womanizings into rational respectability, with its attendant moral obtuseness. Hippolyta, though championed as a victim by feminist critics, shows little aversion to being wooed by the sword and seems content to dwindle into Athenian domesticity after her exploits with Oberon, though she retains a vision all her own, as will be seen. What Titania magnificently goes on to tell us is that discord between herself and Oberon is a disaster for both the natural and the human realm:

*Tita.* These are the forgeries of jealousy:
    And never, since the middle summer's spring,
    Met we on hill, in dale, forest or mead,
    By paved fountain, or by rushy brook,
    Or in the beached margent of the sea,
    To dance our ringlets to the whistling wind,
    But with thy brawls thou hast disturb'd our sport.
    Therefore the winds, piping to us in vain,
    As in revenge have suck'd up from the sea
    Contagious fogs; which, falling in the land,
    Hath every pelting river made so proud
    That they have overborne their continents.
    The ox hath therefore stretch'd his yoke in vain,
    The ploughman lost his sweat, and the green corn
    Hath rotted ere his youth attain'd a beard;
    The fold stands empty in the drowned field,
    And crows are fatted with the murrion flock;
    The nine-men's-morris is fill'd up with mud,
    And the quaint mazes in the wanton green
    For lack of tread are undistinguishable.
    The human mortals want their winter cheer:
    No night is now with hymn or carol blest.
    Therefore the moon, the governess of floods,
    Pale in her anger, washes all the air,
    That rheumatic diseases do abound.
    And thorough this distemperature we see
    The seasons alter: hoary-headed frosts
    Fall in the fresh lap of the crimson rose;
    And on old Hiems' thin and icy crown,

An odorous chaplet of sweet summer buds
Is, as in mockery, set; the spring, the summer,
The childing autumn, angry winter, change
Their wonted liveries; and the mazed world,
By their increase, now knows not which is which.
And this same progeny of evils comes
From our debate, from our dissension;
We are their parents and original.

[II.i.81–117]

No previous poetry by Shakespeare achieved this extraordinary quality; he finds here one of his many authentic voices, the paean of natural lament. Power in the *Dream* is magical rather than political; Theseus is ignorant when he assigns power to the paternal, or to masculine sexuality. Our contemporary heirs of the materialist metaphysics of Iago, Thersites, and Edmund see Oberon as only another assertion of masculine authority, but they need to ponder Titania's lamentation. Oberon is superior in trickery, since he controls Puck, and he will win Titania back to what he considers his kind of amity. But is that a reassertion of male dominance, or of something much subtler? The issue between the fairy queen and king is a custody dispute: "I do but beg a little changeling boy / To be my henchman"— that is, Oberon's page of honor in his court. Rather than the unbounded prurience that many critics insist upon, I see nothing but an innocent assertion of sovereignty in Oberon's whim, or in Titania's poignant and beautiful refusal to yield up the child:

Set your heart at rest:
The fairy land buys not the child of me.
His mother was a votress of my order;

And in the spiced Indian air, by night,
Full often hath she gossip'd by my side;
And sat with me on Neptune's yellow sands,
Marking th'embarked traders on the flood:
When we have laugh'd to see the sails conceive
And grow big-bellied with the wanton wind;
Which she, with pretty and with swimming gait
Following (her womb then rich with my young squire),
Would imitate, and sail upon the land
To fetch me trifles, and return again
As from a voyage rich with merchandise.
But she, being mortal, of that boy did die;
And for her sake do I rear up her boy;
And for her sake I will not part with him.

[II.i.121–37]

Ruth Nevo accurately observes that Titania has so assimilated her votaries to herself that the changeling child has become her own, in a relationship that firmly excludes Oberon. To make the boy his henchman would be an assertion of adoption, like Prospero's initial stance toward Caliban, and Oberon will utilize Puck to achieve this object. But why should Oberon, who is not jealous of Theseus, and is willing to be cuckolded by Titania's enchantment, feel so fiercely in regard to the changeling's custody? Shakespeare will not tell us, and so we must interpret this ellipsis for ourselves.

One clear implication is that Oberon and Titania have no male child of their own; Oberon being immortal need not worry about an heir, but evidently he has paternal aspirations that his henchman Puck cannot satisfy. It may also be relevant that the changeling boy's father was an Indian king, and that tradition traces Oberon's royal lineage to an Indian emperor. What matters most appears to be Titania's refusal to allow Oberon any share in her adoption of the child. Perhaps David Wiles is correct in arguing that Oberon desires to parallel the pattern of Elizabethan aristocratic marriages, where the procreation of a male heir was the highest object, though Elizabeth herself as Virgin Queen undoes the tradition, and Elizabeth is the ultimate patroness of the *Dream*.

I think the quarrel between Titania and Oberon is subtler, and turns on the question of the links between mortals and immortals in the play. Theseus's and Hippolyta's amours with the fairies are safely in the past, and Oberon and Titania, however estranged from each other, have arrived in the wood near Athens to bless the wedding of their former lovers. Bottom, one of the least likely of mortals, will sojourn briefly among the fairies, but his metamorphosis, when it comes, is merely outward. The Indian child is a true changeling; he will live out his life among the immortals. That is anything but irrelevant to Oberon: he and his subjects have their mysteries, jealously guarded from mortals. To exclude Oberon from the child's company is therefore not just a challenge to male authority; it is a wrong done to Oberon, and one that he must reverse and subsume in the name of the legitimacy in leadership that he shares with Titania. As Oberon says, it is an "injury."

To torment Titania away from her resolution, Oberon invokes what becomes the most beautiful of Shakespeare's visions in the play:

> *Obe.*          Thou rememb'rest
>   Since once I sat upon a promontory,
>   And heard a mermaid on a dolphin's back
>   Uttering such dulcet and harmonious breath
>   That the rude sea grew civil at her song

And certain stars shot madly from their spheres
  To hear the sea maid's music?
*Puck.*                    I remember.
*Obe.* That very time I saw (but thou couldst not),
  Flying between the cold moon and the earth,
  Cupid all arm'd: a certain aim he took
  At a fair vestal, throned by the west,
  And loos'd his love-shaft smartly from his bow
  As it should pierce a hundred thousand hearts.
  But I might see young Cupid's fiery shaft
  Quench'd in the chaste beams of the watery moon;
  And the imperial votress passed on,
  In maiden meditation, fancy-free.
  Yet mark'd I where the bolt of Cupid fell:
  It fell upon a little western flower,
  Before milk-white, now purple with love's wound:
  And maidens call it 'love-in-idleness'.
  Fetch me that flower; the herb I show'd thee once.
  The juice of it, on sleeping eyelids laid,
  Will make or man or woman madly dote
  Upon the next live creature that it sees.
  Fetch me this herb, and be thou here again
  Ere the leviathan can swim a league.
*Puck.* I'll put a girdle round about the earth
  In forty minutes.
*Obe.*             Having once this juice.
  I'll watch Titania when she is asleep,
  And drop the liquor of it in her eyes:
  The next thing then she waking looks upon
  (Be it on lion, bear, or wolf, or bull,
  On meddling monkey, or on busy ape)
  She shall pursue it with the soul of love.

And ere I take this charm from off her sight
(As I can take it with another herb)
I'll make her render up her page to me.

[II.i.148–85]

The flower love-in-idleness is the pansy; the "fair vestal, throned by the west" is Queen Elizabeth I, and one function of this fairy vision is to constitute Shakespeare's largest and most direct tribute to his monarch during her lifetime. She passes on, and remains fancy-free; the arrow of Cupid, unable to wound the Virgin Queen, instead converts the pansy into a universal love charm. It is as though Elizabeth's choice of chastity opens up a cosmos of erotic possibilities for others, but at the high cost of accident and arbitrariness replacing her reasoned choice. Love at first sight, exalted in *Romeo and Juliet,* is pictured here as calamity. The ironic possibilities of the love elixir are first intimated when, in one of the play's most exquisite passages, Oberon plots the ensnarement of Titania:

I know a bank where the wild thyme blows,
Where oxlips and the nodding violet grows,
Quite over-canopied with luscious woodbine,
With sweet musk-roses, and with eglantine.
There sleeps Titania sometime of the night,
Lull'd in these flowers with dances and delight;
And there the snake throws her enamell'd skin,
Weed wide enough to wrap a fairy in;
And with the juice of this I'll streak her eyes,
And make her full of hateful fantasies.

[II.i.249–58]

The contrast between those first six lines and the four that come after grants us an aesthetic *frisson*; the transition is from Keats and Tennyson to Browning and the early T. S. Eliot, as Oberon modulates from sensuous naturalism to grotesque gusto. Shakespeare thus prepares the way for the play's great turning point in Act III, Scene i, where Puck transforms Bottom, and Titania wakens with the great outcry, "What angel wakes me from my flowery bed?" The angel is the imperturbable Bottom, who is sublimely undismayed that his amiable countenance has metamorphosed into an ass head.

This wonderfully comic scene deserves pondering: Who among us could sustain so weird a calamity with so equable a spirit? One feels that Bottom could have undergone the fate of Kafka's Gregor Samsa with only moderate chagrin. He enters almost on cue, chanting, "If I were fair, Thisbe, I were only thine," scattering his fellows. Presumably discouraged at his inability to frighten Bottom, the frustrated Puck chases after the Mechanicals, taking on many fearsome guises. Our bully Bottom responds to Peter Quince's "Bless thee, Bottom, bless thee! Thou art translated," by cheerfully singing a ditty hinting at cuckoldry, thus preparing us for a comic dialogue that even Shakespeare was never to surpass:

> *Tita.* I pray thee, gentle mortal, sing again:
> Mine ear is much enamour'd of thy note;
> So is mine eye enthralled to thy shape;
> And thy fair virtue's force perforce doth move me
> On the first view to say, to swear, I love thee.
> *Bot.* Methinks, mistress, you should have little reason for
> that. And yet, to say the truth, reason and love keep lit-
> tle company together nowadays. The more the pity that
> some honest neighbours will not make them friends.
> Nay, I can gleek upon occasion.
> *Tita.* Thou art as wise as thou art beautiful.

*Bot.* Not so neither; but if I had wit enough to get out of
  this wood, I have enough to serve my own turn.
*Tita.* Out of this wood do not desire to go:
  Thou shalt remain here, whether thou wilt or no.

[III.i.132–46]

Even C. L. Barber somewhat underestimates Bottom, when he
says that Titania and Bottom are "fancy against fact," since "enchantment against Truth" is more accurate. Bottom is unfailingly
courteous, courageous, kind, and sweet-tempered, and he humors
the beautiful queen whom he clearly knows to be quite mad. The
ironies here are fully in Bottom's control, and are kept gentle by
his tact. Nothing else in the *Dream* is as pithy an account of its
erotic confusions: "reason and love keep little company together
nowadays." Bottom too can "gleek" (jest) upon occasion, which
is the only other possibility, should poor Titania prove to be sane.
Neither wise nor beautiful, Bottom sensibly wishes to get out of
the wood, but he does not seem particularly alarmed when Titania tells him he is a prisoner. Her proud assertion of rank and self
is hilarious in its absurd confidence that she can purge Bottom's
"mortal grossness" and transform him into another "airy spirit,"
as though he could be another changeling like the Indian boy:

*Tita.* I am a spirit of no common rate;
  The summer still doth tend upon my state;
  And I do love thee: therefore go with me.
  I'll give thee fairies to attend on thee;
  And they shall fetch thee jewels from the deep,
  And sing, while thou on pressed flowers dost sleep:
  And I will purge thy mortal grossness so,
  That thou shalt like an airy spirit go.
  Peaseblossom! Cobweb! Moth! And Mustardseed!

[III.i.147–55]

Bottom, amiable enough to the infatuated Titania, is truly charmed by the four elves, and they by Bottom, who would be one of them even without benefit of Puckish translation:

*Peas.* Ready.

*Cob.* And I.

*Moth.* And I.

*Mus.* And I.

*All.* Where shall we go?

*Tita.* Be kind and courteous to this gentleman;
    Hop in his walks, and gambol in his eyes;
    Feed him with apricocks and dewberries,
    With purple grapes, green figs, and mulberries;
    The honey-bags steal from the humble-bees,
    And for night-tapers crop their waxen thighs,
    And light them at the fiery glow-worms' eyes,
    To have my love to bed, and to arise;
    And pluck the wings from painted butterflies
    To fan the moonbeams from his sleeping eyes.
    Nod to him, elves, and do him courtesies.

*Peas.* Hail, mortal!

*Cob.* Hail!

*Moth.* Hail!

*Mus.* Hail!

*Bot.* I cry your worships mercy, heartily. I beseech your
    worship's name?

*Cob.* Cobweb.

*Bot.* I shall desire you of more acquaintance, good Master
    Cobweb: if I cut my finger, I shall make bold with you.
    Your name, honest gentleman?

*Peas.* Peaseblossom.

*Bot.* I pray you, commend me to Mistress Squash, your
    mother, and to Master Peascod, your father. Good Master

> Peaseblossom, I shall desire you of more acquaintance
> too. Your name, I beseech you sir?
> *Mus.* Mustardseed.
> *Bot.* Good Master Mustardseed, I know your patience
> well. That same cowardly giant-like ox-beef hath de-
> voured many a gentleman of your house: I promise
> you, your kindred hath made my eyes water ere now. I
> desire you of more acquaintance, good Master
> Mustardseed.
>
> > [III.i.156–89]

Though Titania will follow this colloquy of innocents by order-
ing the elves to lead Bottom to her bower, it remains ambiguous
exactly what transpires there amidst the nodding violet, luscious
woodbine, and sweet musk roses. If you are not Jan Kott or Peter
Brook, does it matter? Does one remember the play for "orgiastic
bestiality" or for Peaseblossom, Cobweb, Moth, and Mustardseed?
Undoubtedly played by children then, as they are now, these elves
are adept at stealing from honeybees and butterflies, a precarious art
emblematic of the entire *Dream*. Bottom's grave courtesy to them
and their cheerful attentiveness to him help establish an affinity that
suggests what is profoundly childlike (not childish, not bestial)
about Bottom. The problem with reacting to resenters is that I
sometimes hear the voice of my late mentor, Frederick A. Pottle,
of Yale, admonishing me: "Mr. Bloom, stop beating dead wood-
chucks!" I will do so, and am content to cite Empson on Kott:

> I take my stand beside the other old buffers here. Kott is
> ridiculously indifferent to the Letter of the play and labors
> to befoul its spirit.

Fairies in general (Puck in particular) are likely to miss one tar-
get and hit another. Instructed by Oberon to divert Demetrius's

passion from Hermia to Helena, Puck errs and transforms Lysander into Helena's pursuer. When Puck gets it right at second try, the foursome become more absurd than ever, with Helena, believing herself mocked, fleeing both suitors, while Hermia languishes in a state of amazement. Act III concludes with all four exhausted lovers being put to sleep by Puck, who carefully rearranges Lysander's affections to their original object, Hermia, while keeping Demetrius enthralled by Helena. This raises the happy irony that the play will never resolve: Does it make any difference at all who marries whom? Shakespeare's pragmatic answer is: Not much, whether in this comedy or another, since all marriages seem in Shakespeare to be headed for unhappiness. Shakespeare seems always to hold what I call the "black box" theory of object choice. The airliner goes down, and we seek out the black box to learn the cause of the catastrophe, but our black boxes are unfindable, and our marital disasters are as arbitrary as our successes. Perhaps this should be called "Puck's Law": who can say whether Demetrius-Helena or Lysander-Hermia will prove the better match? Act III of the *Dream* brushes aside any such question, ending as it does with Puck singing:

> Jack shall have Jill,
> Nought shall go ill.

[III.ii.461–62]

# 4

Everyone should collect favorite acts in Shakespeare; one of mine would be Act IV of the *Dream,* where wonder crowds wonder and eloquence overflows, as Shakespeare manifests his creative exuberance without pause. The orgiastic reading is prophetically dismissed by the first scene, where Titania sits the amiable Bottom down upon a flowery bed, caresses his cheeks, sticks musk roses in his head, and kisses his ears. This scarcely arouses Bottom to lust:

*Bot.* Where's Peaseblossom?

*Peas.* Ready.

*Bot.* Scratch my head, Peaseblossom. Where's Mounsieur Cobweb?

*Cob.* Ready.

*Bot.* Mounsieur Cobweb, good mounsieur, get you your weapons in your hand, and kill me a red-hipped humble-bee on the top of a thistle; and good mounsieur, bring me the honey-bag. Do not fret yourself too much in the action, mounsieur; and good mounsieur, have a care the honey-bag break not; I would be loath to have you overflowen with a honey-bag, signior. Where's Mounsieur Mustardseed?

*Mus.* Ready.

*Bot.* Give me your neaf, Mounsieur Mustardseed. Pray you, leave your courtesy, good mounsieur.

*Mus.* What's your will?

*Bot.* Nothing, good mounsieur, but to help Cavalery Cobweb to scratch. I must to the barber's, mounsieur, for methinks I am marvellous hairy about the face; and I am such a tender ass, if my hair do but tickle me, I must scratch.

*Tita.* What, wilt thou hear some music, my sweet love?

*Bot.* I have a reasonable good ear in music. Let's have the tongs and the bones.

*Tita.* Or say, sweet love, what thou desir'st to eat?

*Bot.* Truly, a peck of provender; I could munch your good

dry oats. Methinks I have a great desire to a bottle of
hay: good hay, sweet hay, hath no fellow.

[IV.i.5–33]

What hath Puck wrought: for Titania, a considerable indig-
nity, no doubt, but for Bottom a friendship with four elves. Since
Bottom is getting drowsy, we can understand his mixing up
Cobweb with Peaseblossom, but he is otherwise much himself,
even if his eating habits perforce are altered. He falls asleep, en-
twined with the rapt Titania, in a charmingly innocent embrace.
Oberon informs us that, since she has surrendered the changeling
boy to him, all is forgiven so that Puck can cure her enchantment, and in passing, Bottom's, though the weaver resolutely
goes on sleeping. Shakespeare's touch here is astonishingly light;
metamorphoses are represented by the dance of reconciliation
that restores the marriage of Oberon and Titania:

Come my queen, take hands with me,
And rock the ground whereon these sleepers be.

[IV.i.84–85]

The four lovers and Bottom stay fast asleep even as Theseus,
Hippolyta, and their train make a boisterous entry with a dialogue
that is Shakespeare's bravura defense of his art of fusion in this play:

*The.* Go one of you, find out the forester;
For now our observation is perform'd,
And since we have the vaward of the day,
My love shall hear the music of my hounds.
Uncouple in the western valley; let them go;
Dispatch I say, and find the forester.

*Exit an* Attendant.

> We will, fair queen, up to the mountain's top,
> And mark the musical confusion
> Of hounds and echo in conjunction.
> *Hip.* I was with Hercules and Cadmus once,
> When in a wood of Crete they bay'd the bear
> With hounds of Sparta; never did I hear
> Such gallant chiding; for, besides the groves,
> The skies, the fountains, every region near
> Seem'd all one mutual cry; I never heard
> So musical a discord, such sweet thunder.
> *The.* My hounds are bred out of the Spartan kind,
> So flew'd, so sanded; and their heads are hung
> With ears that sweep away the morning dew;
> Crook-knee'd and dewlapp'd like Thessalian bulls;
> Slow in pursuit, but match'd in mouth like bells,
> Each under each: a cry more tuneable
> Was never holla'd to, nor cheer'd with horn,
> In Crete, in Sparta, nor in Thessaly.
> Judge when you hear. But soft, what nymphs are these?
> [IV.i.102–26]

The musical discord holds together four different modes of representation: Theseus and Hippolyta, from classical legend; the four young lovers, from every place and every time; Bottom and his fellow English rustics; the fairies, who in themselves are madly eclectic. Titania is Ovid's alternate name for Diana, while Oberon comes out of Celtic romance, and Puck or Robin Goodfellow is English folklore. In their delightfully insane dialogue, Theseus and Hippolyta join in celebrating the wonderful nonsense of the Spartan hounds, bred only for their baying, so that they are "slow in pursuit." Shakespeare celebrates the "sweet thunder" of his comic extravagance, which like Theseus's hounds is in no particular hurry to get anywhere, and which still has superb surprises for us. I pass over the awakening of the four lovers (Demetrius now in love with Helena) to come at the finest speech Shakespeare had yet written, Bottom's sublime reverie upon waking up:

> *Bot.* When my cue comes, call me and I will answer. My
> next is 'Most fair Pyramus'. Heigh-ho! Peter Quince?
> Flute, the bellows-mender? Snout, the tinker?
> Starveling? God's my life! Stolen hence, and left me
> asleep! I have had a most rare vision. I have had a dream,
> past the wit of man to say what dream it was. Man is
> but an ass if he go about to expound this dream.
> Methought I was—there is no man can tell what.
> Methought I was—and methought I had—but man is
> but a patched fool if he will offer to say what
> methought I had. The eye of man hath not heard, the
> ear of man hath not seen, man's hand is not able to
> taste, his tongue to conceive, nor his heart to report,
> what my dream was. I will get Peter Quince to write a
> ballad of this dream: it shall be called 'Bottom's
> Dream', because it hath no bottom; and I will sing it in
> the latter end of a play, before the Duke. Peradventure,
> to make it the more gracious, I shall sing it at her death.
> [IV.i.199–217]

"The Spirite searcheth . . . the botome of Goddes secretes," is the Geneva Bible's rendering of 1 Corinthians 2:9–10. Bottom's parody of 1 Corinthians 2:9 is audacious, and allows Shakespeare to anticipate William Blake's Romantic vision, with its repudiation of the Pauline split between flesh and spirit, though Bottom seems to have heard the text preached to him in the Bishops' Bible version:

The eye hath not seene, and the eare hath not heard, neyther have entered into the heart of man, the things which God hath purposed . . .

For Bottom, "the eye . . . hath not heard, the ear . . . hath not seen, [the] hand is not able to taste, his tongue to conceive, nor his heart to report" the truths of his bottomless dream. Like William Blake after him, Bottom suggests an apocalyptic, unfallen man, whose awakened senses fuse in a synesthetic unity. It is difficult not to find in Bottom, in this his sublimest moment, an ancestor not just of Blake's Albion but of Joyce's Earwicker, the universal dreamer of *Finnegans Wake*. Bottom's greatness—Shakespeare upon his heights—emerges most strongly in what could be called "Bottom's Vision," a mysterious triumph he is to enjoy before Theseus as audience, where the "play" cannot be the mere travesty, the play-within-the-play *Pyramus and Thisbe*:

I will get Peter Quince to write a ballad of this dream: it shall be called 'Bottom's Dream', because it hath no bottom; and I will sing it in the latter end of a play, before the Duke. Peradventure, to make it the more gracious, I shall sing it at her death.

Whose death? Since we do not know the visionary drama playing out in Bottom's consciousness, we cannot answer the question, except to say that it is neither Titania nor Thisbe. When, in the next scene, sweet bully Bottom returns joyously to his friends, he will not speak in these tones. Shakespeare, though, has not forgotten this "more gracious" aspect of Bottom, and subtly opposes it to the famous speech of Theseus that opens Act V. Hippolyta muses on the strangeness of the story told by the four young lovers, and Theseus opposes his skepticism to her wonder.

> *The.* More strange than true. I never may believe
> These antique fables, nor these fairy toys.
> Lovers and madmen have such seething brains,
> Such shaping fantasies, that apprehend
> More than cool reason ever comprehends.
> The lunatic, the lover, and the poet
> Are of imagination all compact:
> One sees more devils than vast hell can hold;
> That is the madman: the lover, all as frantic,
> Sees Helen's beauty in a brow of Egypt:
> The poet's eye, in a fine frenzy rolling,
> Doth glance from heaven to earth, from earth to
>       heaven;
> And as imagination bodies forth
> The forms of things unknown, the poet's pen
> Turns them to shapes, and gives to airy nothing
> A local habitation and a name.
> Such tricks hath strong imagination,
> That if it would but apprehend some joy,
> It comprehends some bringer of that joy:
> Or, in the night, imagining some fear,
> How easy is a bush suppos'd a bear!
>
>                              [V.i.2–22]

Theseus himself could be called, not unkindly, "highly unimaginative," but there are two voices here, and one perhaps is Shakespeare's own, half-distancing itself from its own art, though declining also to yield completely to the patronizing Theseus. When Shakespeare writes these lines, the lover sees Helen's beauty

in a gypsy girl's brow, and yet the prophetic consciousness some-
where in Shakespeare anticipates Antony seeing Helen's beauty
in Cleopatra. "Imagination," to Shakespeare's contemporaries,
was "fantasy," a powerful but suspect faculty of the mind. Sir
Francis Bacon neatly stated this ambiguity:

> Neither is the Imagination simply and only a messenger;
> but is invested with or at leastwise usurpeth no small au-
> thority in itself, besides the duty of the message.

"Usurpeth" is the key word there; the mind for Bacon is the
legitimate authority, and imagination should be content to be the
mind's messenger, and to assert no authority for itself. Theseus is
more a Baconian than a Shakespearean, but Hippolyta breaks
away from Theseus's dogmatism:

> But all the story of the night told over,
> And all their minds transfigur'd so together,
> More witnesseth than fancy's images,
> And grows to something of great constancy;
> But howsoever, strange and admirable.
>
> [V.i.23–27]

You could give Hippolyta's lines a rather minimal interpreta-
tion, stressing that she herself distrusts "fancy's images," but that
seems to me a woeful reading. For Theseus, poetry is a furor, and
the poet a trickster; Hippolyta opens to a greater resonance, to
transfiguration that affects more than one mind at once. The lovers
are her metaphor for the Shakespearean audience, and it is ourselves, therefore, who grow into "something of great constancy,"
and so are re-formed, strangely and admirably. Hippolyta's majes-
tic gravity is an implicit rebuke to Theseus's scoffing at the poet's
"fine frenzy." Critics rightly have expanded their apprehension of

Shakespeare's "story of the night" beyond the *Dream,* marvelous as the play is. "No, I assure you; the wall is down that parted their fathers" is Bottom's final resonance in the play, and transcends Theseus's patronizing understanding. "The best in this kind are but shadows," Theseus says of all plays and playing—and while we might accept this from Macbeth, we cannot accept it from the dull Duke of Athens. Puck, in the Epilogue, only seems to agree with Theseus when he chants that "we shadows" are "but a dream," since the dream is this great play itself. The poet who dreamed Bottom was about to achieve a great dream of reality, Sir John Falstaff, who would have no interest in humoring Theseus.

william shakespeare

# a midsummer night's dream

# synopsis

The marriage of the heroic Theseus, Duke of Athens, to Hippolyta, Queen of the Amazons, is to take place at the next new moon, and he requests his master of ceremonies, Philostrate, to urge the Athenian youths to participate in the fortnight's revels that will follow the wedding.

A group of simple, untutored craftsmen, anxious to entertain the royal couple, meet to select parts in a play which is their own version of the story of Pyramus and Thisbe, and plan to hold a rehearsal in the woods at the Duke's oak. Just at this time, the Duke is called upon by a prominent citizen, Egeus, to evoke the old Athenian law which will force his daughter Hermia to marry the man of her father's choice, Demetrius, or accept the alternative of death or life in a convent. The Duke upholding the law, Hermia and Lysander, the man she loves, arrange in desperation to meet in the wood the following night and escape to the home of the youth's aunt where they will be married. They make the mistake, however, of confiding in Hermia's friend Helena who, in love with Demetrius, warns him of the elopement in a foolish endeavor to win his favor and in order to follow him in his chase after the runaway pair.

The wood which is the destination of both the lovers and the craftsmen is filled with fairies who have come from India to wish joy and prosperity to Theseus and Hippolyta, but at the present moment they are seriously disturbed by a quarrel between Oberon, the King, and his Queen Titania, over the custody of a little changeling boy whom the Queen insists upon rearing, while the King wants him for his henchman. Oberon suddenly recalls having seen Cupid aim at a fair vestal with one of his swift arrows which, missing fire, fell on a little milk-white flower, turning it purple. He sends his hobgoblin, Puck, on a hasty search of the world for the flower, the juice of which when dropped on the eyelids of any sleeper will make the victim dote foolishly on the first creature he sees when awakening, and he plans to embarrass Titania by causing her to fall in love with some monstrosity while he gains possession of the changeling.

Demetrius now appears, seeking for the eloping lovers, with Helena closely following, and the fairy king, perceiving the young man's scorn for the girl, instructs Puck upon his return a little later to squeeze the fatal juice into the youth's eyes, whom the hobgoblin is to recognize by his Athenian clothes. Through Puck's error, Lysander, sleeping on the ground near Hermia, is anointed, awakens to see Helena still in pursuit of Demetrius, makes violent love to her, and follows her into the wood. Hermia wakes up and goes in search of Lysander, only to meet Demetrius whom she accuses of murdering her lover. After a while Demetrius, exhausted, lies down to sleep, and Oberon, having learned of Puck's mistake, sends his messenger to fetch Helena while he drops the love-potion into Demetrius' eyes. As Helena comes to the spot, quarreling with Lysander, the noise awakens Demetrius who falls in love with the girl in rivalry with Lysander, and when Hermia arrives, the confusion deepens and bitter words are exchanged on all sides, with the young men rushing out at length to fight a duel. Puck sets things straight, however, by intercepting the duellists, causing the four lovers to fall asleep, and removing the spell from Lysander's eyes with the juice of another flower.

Meanwhile the craftsmen meet in the wood near the fairy queen's abode, and the knavish Puck gleefully watches his chance to slip an ass's head upon the foolish Nick Bottom's shoulders. The rest of the company flee in terror at the sight and Titania wakes up, falls violently in love with the absurd monster, adorns his head with musk-roses, orders her fairies to wait upon him and fetch him fairy food, and falls asleep in his arms. Oberon, having achieved his purpose in carrying off the changeling boy, cures her enchantment and orders Puck to release the ass's head as Bottom wakes up, stretches himself and thinks it all a rare dream.

At the break of day Theseus, Hippolyta and their train come to the wood to hunt and awaken the lovers with their horns. When the Duke finds that Demetrius, being in love with Helena, willingly gives up Hermia to Lysander, he is so pleased that he invites the lovers to be married in the same ceremony with himself and Hippolyta. Festivities hold full sway in Athens for two weeks after the wedding, and one night the list of revels includes the craftsmen's play against which Philostrate, master of ceremonies, protests saying it is laughably crude. The Duke reminds him that when duty and simpleness tender anything it is never amiss, and he graciously requests the performance of Pyramus and Thisbe.

Leaving nothing to the imagination, the craftsmen present an actor to represent the lion, another the moonshine, and yet another the wall which holds up its fingers to allow Pyramus to peer through at Thisbe. The craftsmen close their entertainment with a dance and leave well pleased with themselves and their reception. At midnight Oberon and Titania with their fairy train sweep through the palace, dancing and singing, and when they have blessed the sleepers they vanish.

## historical data

A variety of sources supplied Shakespeare with the material which he blended together in the harmonious and original world of faery in *A Midsummer Night's Dream*. North's translation of Plutarch's *Lives* and Chaucer's *Knight's Tale* furnished the chief suggestions for Theseus and Hippolyta and their marriage. Golding's translation of Ovid's *Metamorphoses* and Chaucer's *Wife of Bath's Tale* gave him his characterization of Titania, which name was also one of Ovid's variants of Diana. Oberon appears in mediæval romances such as *Huon of Bordeaux* (1534), Greene's *James IV,* in the *Faerie Queen,* and elsewhere. Chaucer's *Merchant's Tale* probably was the source of the Fairy King and Queen's quarrel, while Monte-mayor's *Diana Enamorada* may have suggested the love-potion flower. The story of Pyramis and Thisbe is found both in Chaucer and in Ovid.

The comedy may have been written in celebration of the marriage of some nobleman (sometimes identified as the Earl of Derby who espoused Elizabeth Vere at the Court at Greenwich in 1594) but a reasonable opinion indicates that it was probably written for a performance on the festival of St. John, "Midsummer's Night," just as *Twelfth Night* was prepared for performance on that Winter festival.

From Titania's description of the cold summer (of 1594)

authorities are inclined to the year 1594 as the probable date of the comedy. It is included by Meres in his compilation of 1598 and was first published in quarto edition in 1600.

# dramatis personæ

Theseus, *Duke of Athens.*

Egeus, *father to Hermia.*

Lysander, } *in love with Hermia.*
Demetrius,

Philostrate, *master of the revels to Theseus.*

Quince, *a carpenter.*

Snug, *a joiner.*

Bottom, *a weaver.*

Flute, *a bellows-mender.*

Snout, *a tinker.*

Starveling, *a tailor.*

Hippolyta, *queen of the Amazons, betrothed to Theseus.*

Hermia, *daughter to Egeus, in love with Lysander.*

Helena, *in love with Demetrius.*

Oberon, *king of the fairies.*

Titania, *queen of the fairies.*

Puck, *or Robin Goodfellow.*

Peaseblossom, }
Cobweb, } *fairies.*
Moth, }
Mustardseed, }

Other Fairies *attending their King and Queen. Attendants on Theseus and Hippolyta.*

*Scene:* Athens, and a wood near it.

# act 1

**scene 1.**   [*Athens. The palace of* Theseus]

*Enter* Theseus, Hippolyta, Philostrate, *and* Attendants

*Theseus.* Now, fair Hippolyta, our nuptial hour
    Draws on apace; four happy days bring in
    Another moon: but, O, methinks, how slow
    This old moon wanes! she lingers my desires,
    Like to a step-dame or a dowager
    Long withering out a young man's revenue.

*Hippolyta.* Four days will quickly steep themselves in night;
    Four nights will quickly dream away the time;
    And then the moon, like to a silver bow
    New-bent in heaven, shall behold the night
    Of our solemnities.

*Theseus.*           Go, Philostrate,
    Stir up the Athenian youth to merriments;
    Awake the pert and nimble spirit of mirth:
    Turn melancholy forth to funerals;
    The pale companion is not for our pomp.

                                    *Exit* Philostrate.

Hippolyta, I woo'd thee with my sword,
And won thy love, doing thee injuries;
But I will wed thee in another key,
With pomp, with triumph and with revelling.

      *Enter* Egeus, Hermia, Lysander, *and* Demetrius

*Egeus.* Happy be Theseus, our renowned duke!

*Theseus.* Thanks, good Egeus: what's the news with thee?

*Egeus.* Full of vexation come I, with complaint
Against my child, my daughter Hermia.
Stand forth, Demetrius. My noble lord,
This man hath my consent to marry her.
Stand forth, Lysander: and, my gracious duke,
This man hath bewitch'd the bosom of my child:
Thou, thou, Lysander, thou hast given her rhymes,
And interchanged love-tokens with my child:
Thou hast by moonlight at her window sung,
With feigning voice, verses of feigning love;
And stol'n the impression of her fantasy
With bracelets of thy hair, rings, gauds, conceits,
Knacks, trifles, nosegays, sweetmeats, messengers
Of strong prevailment in unharden'd youth:
With cunning hast thou filch'd my daughter's heart,
Turn'd her obedience, which is due to me,
To stubborn harshness: and, my gracious duke,
Be it so she will not here before your Grace
Consent to marry with Demetrius,
I beg the ancient privilege of Athens,
As she is mine, I may dispose of her:
Which shall be either to this gentleman
Or to her death, according to our law
Immediately provided in that case.

*Theseus.* What say you, Hermia? be advised, fair maid:

To you your father should be as a god;
One that composed your beauties; yea, and one
To whom you are but as a form in wax
By him imprinted, and within his power
To leave the figure or disfigure it.
Demetrius is a worthy gentleman.

*Hermia.* So is Lysander.

*Theseus.*                    In himself he is;
But in this kind, wanting your father's voice,
The other must be held the worthier.

*Hermia.* I would my father look'd but with my eyes.

*Theseus.* Rather your eyes must with his judgement look.

*Hermia.* I do entreat your Grace to pardon me.
I know not by what power I am made bold,
Nor how it may concern my modesty
In such a presence here to plead my thoughts;
But I beseech your Grace that I may know
The worst that may befall me in this case,
If I refuse to wed Demetrius.

*Theseus.* Either to die the death, or to abjure
For ever the society of men.
Therefore, fair Hermia, question your desires;
Know of your youth, examine well your blood,
Whether, if you yield not to your father's choice,
You can endure the livery of a nun;
For aye to be in shady cloister mew'd,
To live a barren sister all your life,
Chanting faint hymns to the cold fruitless moon.
Thrice-blessed they that master so their blood,
To undergo such maiden pilgrimage;
But earthlier happy is the rose distill'd

Than that which, withering on the virgin thorn,
Grows, lives, and dies in single blessedness.

*Hermia.* So will I grow, so live, so die, my lord,
Ere I will yield my virgin patent up
Unto his lordship, whose unwished yoke
My soul consents not to give sovereignty.

*Theseus.* Take time to pause; and, by the next new moon—
The sealing-day betwixt my love and me
For everlasting bond of fellowship—
Upon that day either prepare to die
For disobedience to your father's will,
Or else to wed Demetrius, as he would;
Or on Diana's altar to protest
For aye austerity and single life.

*Demetrius.* Relent, sweet Hermia: and Lysander, yield
Thy crazed title to my certain right.

*Lysander.* You have her father's love, Demetrius;
Let me have Hermia's: do you marry him.

*Egeus.* Scornful Lysander! true, he hath my love,
And what is mine my love shall render him.
And she is mine, and all my right of her
I do estate unto Demetrius.

*Lysander.* I am, my lord, as well derived as he,
As well possess'd; my love is more than his;
My fortunes every way as fairly rank'd,
If not with vantage, as Demetrius';
And, which is more than all these boasts can be,
I am beloved of beauteous Hermia:
Why should not I then prosecute my right?
Demetrius, I'll avouch it to his head,
Made love to Nedar's daughter, Helena,

And won her soul; and she, sweet lady, dotes,
Devoutly dotes, dotes in idolatry,
Upon this spotted and inconstant man.

*Theseus.* I must confess that I have heard so much,
And with Demetrius thought to have spoke thereof;
But, being over-full of self-affairs,
My mind did lose it. But, Demetrius, come;
And come, Egeus; you shall go with me,
I have some private schooling for you both.
For you, fair Hermia, look you arm yourself
To fit your fancies to your father's will;
Or else the law of Athens yields you up—
Which by no means we may extenuate—
To death, or to a vow of single life.
Come, my Hippolyta: what cheer, my love?
Demetrius and Egeus, go along:
I must employ you in some business
Against our nuptial, and confer with you
Of something nearly that concerns yourselves.

*Egeus.* With duty and desire we follow you.

*Exeunt all but* Lysander *and* Hermia.

*Lysander.* How now, my love? why is your cheek so pale?
How chance the roses there do fade so fast?

*Hermia.* Belike for want of rain, which I could well
Beteem them from the tempest of my eyes.

*Lysander.* Ay me! for aught that I could ever read,
Could ever hear by tale or history,
The course of true love never did run smooth;
But, either it was different in blood—

*Hermia.* O cross! too high to be enthrall'd to low.

*Lysander.* Or else misgraffed in respect of years—

*Hermia.* O spite! too old to be engaged to young.

*Lysander.* Or else it stood upon the choice of friends—

*Hermia.* O hell! to choose love by another's eyes.

*Lysander.* Or, if there were a sympathy in choice,
War, death, or sickness did lay siege to it,
Making it momentany as a sound,
Swift as a shadow, short as any dream;
Brief as the lightning in the collied night,
That, in a spleen, unfolds both heaven and earth,
And ere a man hath power to say 'Behold!'
The jaws of darkness do devour it up:
So quick bright things come to confusion.

*Hermia.* If then true lovers have been ever cross'd,
It stands as an edict in destiny:
Then let us teach our trial patience,
Because it is a customary cross,
As due to love as thoughts and dreams and sighs,
Wishes and tears, poor fancy's followers.

*Lysander.* A good persuasion: therefore, hear me, Hermia.
I have a widow aunt, a dowager
Of great revenue, and she hath no child:
From Athens is her house remote seven leagues;
And she respects me as her only son.
There, gentle Hermia, may I marry thee;
And to that place the sharp Athenian law
Cannot pursue us. If thou lovest me then,
Steal forth thy father's house to-morrow night;
And in the wood, a league without the town,
Where I did meet thee once with Helena
To do observance to a morn of May,
There will I stay for thee.

*Hermia.*                                    My good Lysander!
  I swear to thee, by Cupid's strongest bow,
  By his best arrow with the golden head,
  By the simplicity of Venus' doves,
  By that which knitteth souls and prospers loves,
  And by that fire which burn'd the Carthage queen
  When the false Troyan under sail was seen,
  By all the vows that ever men have broke
  (In number more than ever women spoke),
  In that same place thou hast appointed me,
  To-morrow truly will I meet with thee.

*Lysander.* Keep promise, love. Look, here comes Helena.

*Enter* Helena

*Hermia.* God speed fair Helena! whither away?

*Helena.* Call you me fair? that fair again unsay.
  Demetrius loves your fair: O happy fair!
  Your eyes are lode-stars; and your tongue's sweet air
  More tuneable than lark to shepherd's ear,
  When wheat is green, when hawthorn buds appear.
  Sickness is catching: O, were favour so,
  Yours would I catch, fair Hermia, ere I go;
  My ear should catch your voice, my eye your eye,
  My tongue should catch your tongue's sweet melody.
  Were the world mine, Demetrius being bated,
  The rest I'ld give to be to you translated.
  O, teach me how you look, and with what art
  You sway the motion of Demetrius' heart!

*Hermia.* I frown upon him, yet he loves me still.

*Helena.* O that your frowns would teach mysmiles such skill!

*Hermia.* I give him curses, yet he gives me love.

*Helena.* O that my prayers could such affection move!

*Hermia.* The more I hate, the more he follows me.

*Helena.* The more I love, the more he hateth me.

*Hermia.* His folly, Helena, is no fault of mine.

*Helena.* None but your beauty: would that fault were mine!

*Hermia.* Take comfort: he no more shall see my face;
 Lysander and myself will fly this place.
 Before the time I did Lysander see,
 Seem'd Athens as a paradise to me:
 O, then what graces in my love do dwell,
 That he hath turn'd a heaven unto a hell!

*Lysander.* Helen, to you our minds we will unfold:
 To-morrow night, when Phœbe doth behold
 Her silver visage in the watery glass,
 Decking with liquid pearl the bladed grass,
 A time that lovers' flights doth still conceal,
 Through Athens' gates have we devised to steal.

*Hermia.* And in the wood, where often you and I
 Upon faint primrose-beds were wont to lie,
 Emptying our bosoms of their counsel sweet,
 There my Lysander and myself shall meet;
 And thence from Athens turn away our eyes,
 To seek new friends and stranger companies.
 Farewell, sweet playfellow: pray thou for us;
 And good luck grant thee thy Demetrius!
 Keep word, Lysander: we must starve our sight
 From lovers' food till morrow deep midnight.

*Lysander.*     I will, my Hermia.

               *Exit* Hermia.

     Helena, adieu:
 As you on him, Demetrius dote on you!

                  *Exit.*

*Helena.* How happy some o'er other some can be!
    Through Athens I am thought as fair as she.
    But what of that? Demetrius thinks not so;
    He will not know what all but he do know:
    And as he errs, doting on Hermia's eyes,
    So I, admiring of his qualities:
    Things base and vile, holding no quantity,
    Love can transpose to form and dignity:
    Love looks not with the eyes, but with the mind;
    And therefore is wing'd Cupid painted blind:
    Nor hath Love's mind of any judgement taste;
    Wings, and no eyes, figure unheedy haste:
    And therefore is Love said to be a child,
    Because in choice he is so oft beguiled.
    As waggish boys in game themselves forswear,
    So the boy Love is perjured everywhere:
    For ere Demetrius look'd on Hermia's eyne,
    He hail'd down oaths that he was only mine;
    And when this hail some heat from Hermia felt,
    So he dissolved, and showers of oaths did melt.
    I will go tell him of fair Hermia's flight:
    Then to the wood will he to-morrow night
    Pursue her; and for this intelligence
    If I have thanks, it is a dear expense:
    But herein mean I to enrich my pain,
    To have his sight thither and back again.

                                            *Exit.*

## scene 2.   [*The same.* Quince's *house*]

*Enter* Quince the Carpenter, Snug the Joiner, Bottom
the Weaver, Flute the Bellows-Mender, Snout the
Tinker, *and* Starveling the Tailor.

*Quince.* Is all our company here?

*Bottom.* You were best to call them generally, man by man,
according to the scrip.

*Quince.* Here is the scroll of every man's name, which is thought
fit, through all Athens, to play in our interlude before the
duke and the duchess, on his wedding-day at night.

*Bottom.* First, good Peter Quince, say what the play treats on;
then read the names of the actors; and so grow to a point.

*Quince.* Marry, our play is, "The most lamentable comedy, and
most cruel death of Pyramus and Thisby."

*Bottom.* A very good piece of work, I assure you, and a merry.
Now, good Peter Quince, call forth your actors by the scroll.
Masters, spread yourselves.

*Quince.* Answer as I call you. Nick Bottom, the weaver.

*Bottom.* Ready. Name what part I am for, and proceed.

*Quince.* You, Nick Bottom, are set down for Pyramus.

*Bottom.* What is Pyramus? a lover, or a tyrant?

*Quince.* A lover, that kills himself most gallant for love.

*Bottom.* That will ask some tears in the true performing of it: if
I do it, let the audience look to their eyes; I will move
storms, I will condole in some measure. To the rest: yet my
chief humour is for a tyrant: I could play Ercles rarely, or a
part to tear a cat in, to make all split.

> The raging rocks
> And shivering shocks
> Shall break the locks
>     Of prison-gates;
> And Phibbus' car
> Shall shine from far,
> And make and mar
>     The foolish Fates.

This was lofty! Now name the rest of the players. This is Ercles' vein, a tyrant's vein; a lover is more condoling.

*Quince.* Francis Flute, the bellows-mender.

*Flute.* Here, Peter Quince.

*Quince.* Flute, you must take Thisby on you.

*Flute.* What is Thisby? a wandering knight?

*Quince.* It is the lady that Pyramus must love.

*Flute.* Nay, faith, let not me play a woman; I have a beard coming.

*Quince.* That's all one: you shall play it in a mask, and you may speak as small as you will.

*Bottom.* An I may hide my face, let me play Thisby too, I'll speak in a monstrous little voice, 'Thisne, Thisne;' 'Ah Pyramus, my lover dear! thy Thisby dear, and lady dear!'

*Quince.* No, no; you must play Pyramus: and, Flute, you Thisby.

*Bottom.* Well, proceed.

*Quince.* Robin Starveling, the tailor.

*Starveling.* Here, Peter Quince.

*Quince.* Robin Starveling, you must play Thisby's mother. Tom Snout, the tinker.

*Snout.* Here, Peter Quince.

*Quince.* You, Pyramus' father: myself, Thisby's father: Snug, the joiner; you, the lion's part: and, I hope, here is a play fitted.

*Snug.* Have you the lion's part written? pray you, if it be, give it me, for I am slow of study.

*Quince.* You may do it extempore, for it is nothing but roaring.

*Bottom.* Let me play the lion too: I will roar, that I will do any man's heart good to hear me; I will roar, that I will make the duke say, 'Let him roar again, let him roar again.'

*Quince.* An you should do it too terribly, you would fright the duchess and the ladies, that they would shriek; and that were enough to hang us all.

*All.* That would hang us, every mother's son.

*Bottom.* I grant you, friends, if you should fright the ladies out of their wits, they would have no more discretion but to hang us: but I will aggravate my voice so, that I will roar you as gently as any sucking dove; I will roar you an 'twere any nightingale.

*Quince.* You can play no part but Pyramus; for Pyramus is a sweet-faced man; a proper man as one shall see in a summer's day; a most lovely, gentleman-like man: therefore you must needs play Pyramus.

*Bottom.* Well, I will undertake it. What beard were I best to play it in?

*Quince.* Why, what you will.

*Bottom.* I will discharge it in either your straw colour beard, your orange-tawny beard, your purple-in-grain beard, or your French-crown-colour beard, your perfect yellow.

*Quince.* Some of your French crowns have no hair at all, and then you will play barefaced. But, masters, here are your parts: and I am to entreat you, request you, and desire you, to con them by to-morrow night; and meet me in the palace wood, a mile without the town, by moonlight; there will we rehearse, for if we meet in the city, we shall be dogged with company, and our devices known. In the meantime I will draw a bill of properties, such as our play wants. I pray you, fail me not.

*Bottom.* We will meet; and there we may rehearse most obscenely and courageously. Take pains; be perfect: adieu.

*Quince.* At the duke's oak we meet.

*Bottom.* Enough; hold or cut bow-strings.

*Exeunt.*

# act 2

## scene 1. [*A wood near Athens*]

*Enter, from opposite sides, a* Fairy, *and* Puck

*Puck.* How now, spirit! whither wander you?

*Fairy.* Over hill, over dale,
    Thorough bush, thorough brier,
Over park, over pale,
    Thorough flood, thorough fire,
I do wander every where,
Swifter than the moon's sphere;
And I serve the fairy queen,
To dew her orbs upon the green.
The cowslips tall her pensioners be:
In their gold coats spots you see;
Those be rubies, fairy favours,
In those freckles live their savours:
I must go seek some dewdrops here,
And hang a pearl in every cowslip's ear.
Farewell, thou lob of spirits; I'll be gone:
Our queen and all her elves come here anon.

*Puck.* The king doth keep his revels here to-night:
Take heed the queen come not within his sight;
For Oberon is passing fell and wrath,
Because that she as her attendant hath
A lovely boy, stolen from an Indian king;
She never had so sweet a changeling:
And jealous Oberon would have the child
Knight of his train, to trace the forests wild;
But she perforce withholds the loved boy,
Crowns him with flowers, and makes him all her joy:
And now they never meet in grove or green,
By fountain clear, or spangled starlight sheen,
But they do square, that all their elves for fear
Creep into acorn cups and hide them there.

*Fairy.* Either I mistake your shape and making quite,
Or else you are that shrewd and knavish sprite
Call'd Robin Goodfellow: are not you he
That frights the maidens of the villagery;
Skim milk, and sometimes labour in the quern,
And bootless make the breathless housewife churn;
And sometime make the drink to bear no barm;
Mislead night-wanderers, laughing at their harm?
Those that Hobgoblin call you, and sweet Puck,
You do their work, and they shall have good luck:
Are not you he?

*Puck.*          Thou speak'st aright;
I am that merry wanderer of the night.
I jest to Oberon, and make him smile,
When I a fat and bean-fed horse beguile,
Neighing in likeness of a filly foal:
And sometime lurk I in a gossip's bowl,
In very likeness of a roasted crab;

And when she drinks, against her lips I bob
And on her withered dewlap pour the ale.
The wisest aunt, telling the saddest tale,
Sometime for three-foot stool mistaketh me;
Then slip I from her bum, down topples she,
And 'tailor' cries, and falls into a cough;
And then the whole quire hold their hips and laugh;
And waxen in their mirth, and neeze, and swear
A merrier hour was never wasted there.
But room, fairy! here comes Oberon.

*Fairy.* And here my mistress. Would that he were gone!
> *Enter, from one side,* Oberon, *with his train;*
> *from the other,* Titania, *with hers*

*Oberon.* Ill met by moonlight, proud Titania.

*Titania.* What, jealous Oberon! Fairies, skip hence:
I have forsworn his bed and company.

*Oberon.* Tarry, rash wanton: am not I thy lord?

*Titania.* Then I must be thy lady: but I know
When thou hast stolen away from fairy land,
And in the shape of Corin sat all day,
Playing on pipes of corn, and versing love
To amorous Phillida. Why art thou here,
Come from the farthest steppe of India?
But that, forsooth, the bouncing Amazon,
Your buskin'd mistress and your warrior love,
To Theseus must be wedded, and you come
To give their bed joy and prosperity.

*Oberon.* How canst thou thus for shame, Titania,
Glance at my credit with Hippolyta,
Knowing I know thy love to Theseus?
Didst thou not lead him through the glimmering night

From Perigenia, whom he ravished?
And make him with fair Ægle break his faith,
With Ariadne and Antiopa?

*Titania.* These are the forgeries of jealousy:
And never, since the middle summer's spring,
Met we on hill, in dale, forest, or mead,
By paved fountain or by rushy brook,
Or in the beached margent of the sea,
To dance our ringlets to the whistling wind,
But with thy brawls thou hast disturb'd our sport.
Therefore the winds, piping to us in vain,
As in revenge have suck'd up from the sea
Contagious fogs; which, falling in the land,
Have every pelting river made so proud,
That they have overborne their continents:
The ox hath therefore stretch'd his yoke in vain,
The ploughman lost his sweat; and the green corn
Hath rotted ere his youth attain'd a beard:
The fold stands empty in the drowned field,
And crows are fatted with the murrion flock;
The nine-men's-morris is fill'd up with mud;
And the quaint mazes in the wanton green,
For lack of tread are undistinguishable:
The human mortals want their winter cheer;
No night is now with hymn or carol blest:
Therefore the moon, the governess of floods,
Pale in her anger, washes all the air,
That rheumatic diseases do abound:
And thorough this distemperature we see
The seasons alter: hoary-headed frosts
Fall in the fresh lap of the crimson rose;
And on old Hiems' thin and icy crown

An odorous chaplet of sweet summer buds
Is, as in mockery, set: the spring, the summer,
The childing autumn, angry winter, change
Their wonted liveries; and the mazed world,
By their increase, now knows not which is which:
And this same progeny of evils comes
From our debate, from our dissension;
We are their parents and original.

*Oberon.* Do you amend it then; it lies in you:
Why should Titania cross her Oberon?
I do but beg a little changeling boy
To be my henchman.

*Titania.*                    Set your heart at rest:
The fairy land buys not the child of me.
His mother was a votaress of my order:
And, in the spiced Indian air, by night,
Full often hath she gossip'd by my side;
And sat with me on Neptune's yellow sands,
Marking th'embarked traders on the flood;
When we have laugh'd to see the sails conceive
And grow big-bellied with the wanton wind;
Which she, with pretty and with swimming gait
Following—her womb then rich with my young squire—
Would imitate, and sail upon the land
To fetch me trifles, and return again
As from a voyage, rich with merchandise.
But she, being mortal, of that boy did die;
And for her sake do I rear up her boy;
And for her sake I will not part with him.

*Oberon.* How long within this wood intend you stay?

*Titania.* Perchance till after Theseus' wedding-day.
If you will patiently dance in our round,

And see our moonlight revels, go with us;
If not, shun me, and I will spare your haunts.

*Oberon.* Give me that boy, and I will go with thee.

*Titania.* Not for thy fairy kingdom. Fairies, away!
We shall chide downright, if I longer stay.

*Exit* Titania *with her train.*

*Oberon.* Well, go thy way: thou shalt not from this grove
Till I torment thee for this injury.
My gentle Puck, come hither. Thou rememberest
Since once I sat upon a promontory,
And heard a mermaid on a dolphin's back
Uttering such dulcet and harmonious breath,
That the rude sea grew civil at her song
And certain stars shot madly from their spheres
To hear the sea–maid's music.

*Puck.*                            I remember.

*Oberon.* That very time I saw, but thou couldst not,
Flying between the cold moon and the earth,
Cupid all arm'd: a certain aim he took
At a fair vestal throned by the west,
And loosed his love-shaft smartly from his bow,
As it should pierce a hundred thousand hearts:
But I might see young Cupid's fiery shaft
Quench'd in the chaste beams of the watery moon,
And the imperial votaress passed on,
In maiden meditation, fancy-free.
Yet mark'd I where the bolt of Cupid fell:
It fell upon a little western flower,
Before milk-white, now purple with love's wound,
And maidens call it "love-in-idleness."
Fetch me that flower; the herb I shew'd thee once.

The juice of it on sleeping eye-lids laid
Will make or man or woman madly dote
Upon the next live creature that it sees.
Fetch me this herb; and be thou here again
Ere the leviathan can swim a league.

*Puck.* I'll put a girdle round about the earth
In forty minutes.

*Oberon.*                    Having once this juice,
I'll watch Titania when she is asleep,
And drop the liquor of it in her eyes.
The next thing then she waking looks upon,
Be it on lion, bear, or wolf, or bull,
On meddling monkey, or on busy ape,
She shall pursue it with the soul of love:
And ere I take this charm from off her sight,
As I can take it with another herb,
I'll make her render up her page to me.
But who comes here? I am invisible;
And I will overhear their conference.

                    *Enter* Demetrius, Helena *following him*

*Demetrius.* I love thee not, therefore pursue me not.
Where is Lysander and fair Hermia?
The one I'll slay, the other slayeth me.
Thou told'st me they were stolen unto this wood;
And here am I, and wode within this wood,
Because I cannot meet my Hermia.
Hence, get thee gone, and follow me no more.

*Helena.* You draw me, you hard-hearted adamant;
But yet you draw not iron, for my heart
Is true as steel: leave you your power to draw,
And I shall have no power to follow you.

*Demetrius.* Do I entice you? do I speak you fair?
   Or, rather, do I not in plainest truth
   Tell you, I do not nor I cannot love you?

*Helena.* And even for that do I love you the more.
   I am your spaniel; and, Demetrius,
   The more you beat me, I will fawn on you:
   Use me but as your spaniel, spurn me, strike me,
   Neglect me, lose me; only give me leave,
   Unworthy as I am, to follow you.
   What worser place can I beg in your love—
   And yet a place of high respect with me—
   Than to be used as you use your dog?

*Demetrius.* Tempt not too much the hatred of my spirit;
   For I am sick when I do look on thee.

*Helena.* And I am sick when I look not on you.

*Demetrius.* You do impeach your modesty too much,
   To leave the city and commit yourself
   Into the hands of one that loves you not;
   To trust the opportunity of night
   And the ill counsel of a desert place
   With the rich worth of your virginity.

*Helena.* Your virtue is my privilege: for that
   It is not night when I do see your face,
   Therefore I think I am not in the night;
   Nor doth this wood lack worlds of company,
   For you in my respect are all the world:
   Then how can it be said I am alone,
   When all the world is here to look on me?

*Demetrius.* I'll run from thee and hide me in the brakes,
   And leave thee to the mercy of wild beasts.

*Helena.* The wildest hath not such a heart as you.
   Run when you will, the story shall be changed:
   Apollo flies, and Daphne holds the chase;
   The dove pursues the griffin; the mild hind
   Makes speed to catch the tiger; bootless speed,
   When cowardice pursues and valour flies.

*Demetrius.* I will not stay thy questions; let me go:
   Or if thou follow me, do not believe
   But I shall do thee mischief in the wood.

*Helena.* Ay, in the temple, in the town, the field,
   You do me mischief. Fie, Demetrius!
   Your wrongs do set a scandal on my sex:
   We cannot fight for love, as men may do;
   We should be woo'd, and were not made to woo.

                           *Exit* Demetrius.

   I'll follow thee, and make a heaven of hell,
   To die upon the hand I love so well.

                                 *Exit.*

*Oberon.* Fare thee well, nymph: ere he do leave this grove,
   Thou shalt fly him, and he shall seek thy love.

                 *Re-enter* Puck.

   Hast thou the flower there? Welcome, wanderer.

*Puck.* Ay, there it is.

*Oberon.*          I pray thee, give it me.
   I know a bank where the wild thyme blows,
   Where oxlips and the nodding violet grows;
   Quite over-canopied with luscious woodbine,
   With sweet musk-roses, and with eglantine:
   There sleeps Titania sometime of the night,
   Lull'd in these flowers with dances and delight;
   And there the snake throws her enamell'd skin,
   Weed wide enough to wrap a fairy in:

And with the juice of this I'll streak her eyes,
And make her full of hateful fantasies.
Take thou some of it, and seek through this grove:
A sweet Athenian lady is in love
With a disdainful youth: anoint his eyes;
But do it when the next thing he espies
May be the lady: thou shalt know the man
By the Athenian garments he hath on.
Effect it with some care that he may prove
More fond on her than she upon her love:
And look thou meet me ere the first cock crow.

*Puck.* Fear not, my lord, your servant shall do so.

*Exeunt.*

## scene 2.   [*Another part of the wood*]

*Enter* Titania, *with her train*

*Titania.* Come, now a roundel and a fairy song;
   Then, for the third part of a minute, hence;
   Some to kill cankers in the musk-rose buds;
   Some war with rere-mice for their leathern wings,
   To make my small elves coats; and some keep back
   The clamorous owl, that nightly hoots and wonders
   At our quaint spirits. Sing me now asleep;
   Then to your offices, and let me rest.

*Song*

*First Fairy.*     You spotted snakes with double tongue,
      Thorny hedgehogs, be not seen;
    Newts and blind-worms, do no wrong,
      Come not near our fairy queen.

*Chorus.*     Philomel, with melody
      Sing in our sweet lullaby;
    Lulla, lulla, lullaby, lulla, lulla, lullaby:

> Never harm, Nor spell, nor charm,
> Come our lovely lady nigh;
> So, good night, with lullaby.

*First Fairy.*    Weaving spiders, come not here;
> Hence, you long-legg'd spinners, hence!
> Beetles black, approach not near;
> Worm nor snail, do no offence.

*Chorus.*    Philomel, with melody, &c.

> Titania *sleeps.*

*Second Fairy.* Hence, away! now all is well:
> One aloof stand sentinel.

> *Exeunt* Fairies.

*Enter* Oberon, *and squeezes the flower on*
Titania's *eyelids*

*Oberon.* What thou seest when thou dost wake,
> Do it for thy true-love take;
> Love and languish for his sake:
> Be it ounce, or cat, or bear,
> Pard, or boar with bristled hair,
> In thy eye that shall appear
> When thou wak'st, it is thy dear:
> Wake when some vile thing is near.

> *Exit.*

*Enter* Lysander *and* Hermia

*Lysander.* Fair love, you faint with wandering in the wood;
> And to speak troth, I have forgot our way:
> We'll rest us, Hermia, if you think it good,
> And tarry for the comfort of the day.

*Hermia.* Be it so, Lysander: find you out a bed;
> For I upon this bank will rest my head.

*Lysander.* One turf shall serve as pillow for us both;
> One heart, one bed, two bosoms, and one troth.

*Hermia.* Nay, good Lysander; for my sake, my dear,
  Lie further off yet, do not lie so near.

*Lysander.* O, take the sense, sweet, of my innocence!
  Love takes the meaning in love's conference.
  I mean that my heart unto yours is knit,
  So that but one heart we can make of it:
  Two bosoms interchained with an oath;
  So then two bosoms and a single troth.
  Then by your side no bed-room me deny;
  For lying so, Hermia, I do not lie.

*Hermia.* Lysander riddles very prettily:
  Now much beshrew my manners and my pride,
  If Hermia meant to say Lysander lied.
  But, gentle friend, for love and courtesy
  Lie further off; in human modesty,
  Such separation as may well be said
  Becomes a virtuous bachelor and a maid,
  So far be distant; and, good night, sweet friend:
  Thy love ne'er alter till thy sweet life end!

*Lysander.* Amen, amen, to that fair prayer, say I;
  And then end life when I end loyalty!
  Here is my bed: sleep give thee all his rest!

*Hermia.* With half that wish the wisher's eyes be press'd!

*They sleep.*

*Enter* Puck

*Puck.* Through the forest have I gone,
  But Athenian found I none,
  On whose eyes I might approve
  This flower's force in stirring love.
  Night and silence.—Who is here?
  Weeds of Athens he doth wear:

This is he, my master said,
Despised the Athenian maid;
And here the maiden, sleeping sound,
On the dank and dirty ground.
Pretty soul! she durst not lie
Near this lack-love, this kill-courtesy.
Churl, upon thy eyes I throw
All the power this charm doth owe.
When thou wakest, let love forbid
Sleep his seat on thy eyelid:
So awake when I am gone;
For I must now to Oberon.

*Exit.*

*Enter* Demetrius *and* Helena, *running*

*Helena.* Stay, though thou kill me, sweet Demetrius.

*Demetrius.* I charge thee, hence, and do not haunt me thus.

*Helena.* O, wilt thou darkling leave me? do not so.

*Demetrius.* Stay, on thy peril: I alone will go.

*Exit.*

*Helena.* O, I am out of breath in this fond chase!
The more my prayer, the lesser is my grace.
Happy is Hermia, wheresoe'er she lies;
For she hath blessed and attractive eyes.
How came her eyes so bright? Not with salt tears:
If so, my eyes are oftener wash'd than hers.
No, no, I am as ugly as a bear;
For beasts that meet me run away for fear:
Therefore no marvel though Demetrius
Do, as a monster, fly my presence thus.
What wicked and dissembling glass of mine
Made me compare with Hermia's sphery eyne?

But who is here? Lysander! on the ground!
Dead? or asleep? I see no blood, no wound.
Lysander, if you live, good sir, awake.

*Lysander.* [*Awaking*] And run through fire I will for thy sweet
    sake.
Transparent Helena! Nature shows art,
That through thy bosom makes me see thy heart.
Where is Demetrius? O, how fit a word
Is that vile name to perish on my sword!

*Helena.* Do not say so, Lysander; say not so.
What though he love your Hermia? Lord, what though?
Yet Hermia still loves you: then be content.

*Lysander.* Content with Hermia! No; I do repent
The tedious minutes I with her have spent.
Not Hermia but Helena I love:
Who will not change a raven for a dove?
The will of man is by his reason sway'd
And reason says you are the worthier maid.
Things growing are not ripe until their season:
So I, being young, till now ripe not to reason;
And touching now the point of human skill,
Reason becomes the marshal to my will,
And leads me to your eyes; where I o'erlook
Love's stories, written in love's richest book.

*Helena.* Wherefore was I to this keen mockery born?
When at your hands did I deserve this scorn?
Is't not enough, is't not enough, young man,
That I did never, no, nor never can,
Deserve a sweet look from Demetrius' eye,
But you must flout my insufficiency?
Good troth, you do me wrong, good sooth, you do,

In such disdainful manner me to woo.
But fare you well: perforce I must confess
I thought you lord of more true gentleness.
O, that a lady, of one man refused,
Should of another therefore be abused!

*Exit.*

*Lysander.* She sees not Hermia. Hermia, sleep thou there:
And never mayst thou come Lysander near!
For as a surfeit of the sweetest things
The deepest loathing to the stomach brings,
Or as the heresies that men do leave
Are hated most of those they did deceive,
So thou, my surfeit and my heresy,
Of all be hated, but the most of me!
And, all my powers, address your love and might
To honour Helen and to be her knight!

*Exit.*

*Hermia.* [*Awaking*] Help me, Lysander, help me! do thy best
To pluck this crawling serpent from my breast!
Ay me, for pity! what a dream was here!
Lysander, look how I do quake with fear:
Methought a serpent eat my heart away,
And you sat smiling at his cruel prey.
Lysander! what, removed? Lysander! lord!
What, out of hearing? gone? no sound, no word?
Alack, where are you? speak, an if you hear;
Speak, of all loves! I swoon almost with fear.
No? then I well perceive you are not nigh:
Either death or you I'll find immediately.

*Exit.*

# act 3

**scene 1.** [*The wood.* Titania *lying asleep*]

*Enter* Quince, Snug, Bottom, Flute, Snout, *and* Starveling

*Bottom.* Are we all met?

*Quince.* Pat, pat; and here's a marvellous convenient place for our rehearsal. This green plot shall be our stage, this hawthorn-brake our tiring-house; and we will do it in action as we will do it before the duke.

*Bottom.* Peter Quince,—

*Quince.* What sayest thou, bully Bottom?

*Bottom.* There are things in this comedy of Pyramus and Thisby that will never please. First, Pyramus must draw a sword to kill himself; which the ladies cannot abide. How answer you that?

*Snout.* By'r lakin, a parlous fear.

*Starveling.* I believe we must leave the killing out, when all is done.

*Bottom.* Not a whit: I have a device to make all well. Write me a prologue; and let the prologue seem to say, we will do no harm with our swords, and that Pyramus is not killed indeed; and, for the more better assurance, tell them that I, Pyramus, am not Pyramus, but Bottom the weaver: this will put them out of fear.

*Quince.* Well, we will have such a prologue; and it shall be written in eight and six.

*Bottom.* No, make it two more; let it be written in eight and eight.

*Snout.* Will not the ladies be afeard of the lion?

*Starveling.* I fear it, I promise you.

*Bottom.* Masters, you ought to consider with yourselves: to bring in,—God shield us!—a lion among ladies is a most dreadful thing; for there is not a more fearful wild-fowl than your lion living: and we ought to look to 't.

*Snout.* Therefore another prologue must tell he is not a lion.

*Bottom.* Nay, you must name his name, and half his face must be seen through the lion's neck; and he himself must speak through, saying thus, or to the same defect—'Ladies,'—or, 'Fair ladies,—I would wish you,'—or, 'I would request you,'—or, 'I would entreat you,—not to fear, not to tremble: my life for yours. If you think I come hither as a lion, it were pity of my life: no, I am no such thing; I am a man as other men are:' and there indeed let him name his name, and tell them plainly, he is Snug the joiner.

*Quince.* Well, it shall be so. But there is two hard things; that is, to bring the moonlight into a chamber; for you know, Pyramus and Thisby meet by moonlight.

*Snout.* Doth the moon shine that night we play our play?

*Bottom.* A calendar, a calendar! look in the almanac; find out moonshine, find out moonshine.

*Quince.* Yes, it doth shine that night.

*Bottom.* Why, then may you leave a casement of the great chamber window, where we play, open, and the moon may shine in at the casement.

*Quince.* Ay; or else one must come in with a bush of thorns and a lantern, and say he comes to disfigure, or to present, the person of moonshine. Then there is another thing: we must have a wall in the great chamber; for Pyramus and Thisby, says the story, did talk through the chink of a wall.

*Snout.* You can never bring in a wall. What say you, Bottom?

*Bottom.* Some man or other must present Wall: and let him have some plaster, or some loam, or some roughcast about him, to signify wall; and let him hold his fingers thus, and through that cranny shall Pyramus and Thisby whisper.

*Quince.* If that may be, then all is well. Come sit down, every mother's son, and rehearse your parts. Pyramus, you begin: when you have spoken your speech, enter into that brake: and so every one according to his cue.

*Enter* Puck *behind*

*Puck.* What hempen home-spuns have we swaggering here,
So near the cradle of the fairy queen?
What, a play toward! I'll be an auditor;
An actor too perhaps, if I see cause.

*Quince.* Speak, Pyramus. Thisby, stand forth.

*Bottom.* Thisby, the flowers of odious savours sweet—

*Quince.* 'Odorous!' 'odorous'!

*Bottom.*      —odours savours sweet:
So hath thy breath, my dearest Thisby dear.
But hark, a voice! stay thou but here awhile,
And by and by I will to thee appear.

*Exit.*

*Puck.* A stranger Pyramus than e'er play'd here.

*Exit.*

*Flute.* Must I speak now?

*Quince.* Ay, marry, must you; for you must understand he goes but to see a noise that he heard, and is to come again.

*Flute.*      Most radiant Pyramus, most lily-white of hue,
            Of colour like the red rose on triumphant brier,
         Most brisky juvenal, and eke most lovely Jew,
            As true as truest horse, that yet would never tire,
         I'll meet thee, Pyramus, at Ninny's tomb.

*Quince.* 'Ninus' tomb,' man: why, you must not speak that yet; that you answer to Pyramus: you speak all your part at once, cues and all. Pyramus, enter: your cue is past; it is 'never tire.'

*Flute.*      O,—As true as truest horse, that yet would never tire.

   *Re-enter* Puck, *and* Bottom *with an ass's head*

*Bottom.*         If I were fair, Thisby, I were only thine.

*Quince.* O monstrous! O strange! we are haunted. Pray, masters! fly, masters! Help!

   *Exeunt* Quince, Snug, Flute, Snout, *and* Starveling.

*Puck.* I'll follow you, I'll lead you about a round,
      Through bog, through bush, through brake, through brier:
   Sometime a horse I'll be, sometime a hound,
      A hog, a headless bear, sometime a fire;
   And neigh, and bark, and grunt, and roar, and burn,
   Like horse, hound, hog, bear, fire, at every turn.

*Exit.*

*Bottom.* Why do they run away? this is a knavery of them to make me afeard.

   *Re-enter* Snout

*Snout.* O Bottom, thou art changed! what do I see on thee?

*Bottom*. What do you see? you see an ass-head of your own, do you?

*Exit* Snout.

*Re-enter* Quince

*Quince*. Bless thee, Bottom! bless thee! thou art translated.

*Exit*.

*Bottom*. I see their knavery: this is to make an ass of me; to fright me, if they could. But I will not stir from this place, do what they can: I will walk up and down here, and I will sing, that they shall hear I am not afraid.

*Sings*.

The ousel cock so black of hue,
With orange-tawny bill,
The throstle with his note so true,
The wren with little quill;

*Titania*. [*Awaking*] What angel wakes me from my flowery bed?

*Bottom*. [*Sings*]

The finch, the sparrow, and the lark,
The plain-song cuckoo gray,
Whose note full many a man doth mark,
And dares not answer nay;—

for, indeed, who would set his wit to so foolish a bird? who would give a bird the lie, though he cry 'cuckoo' never so?

*Titania*. I pray thee, gentle mortal, sing again:
Mine ear is much enamour'd of thy note;
So is mine eye enthralled to thy shape;
And thy fair virtue's force perforce doth move me
On the first view to say, to swear, I love thee.

*Bottom*. Methinks, mistress, you should have little reason for that: and yet, to say the truth, reason and love keep little company together now-a-days; the more the pity, that some honest neighbours will not make them friends. Nay, I can gleek upon occasion.

*Titania.* Thou art as wise as thou art beautiful.

*Bottom.* Not so, neither: but if I had wit enough to get out of
this wood, I have enough to serve mine own turn.

*Titania.* Out of this wood do not desire to go:
Thou shalt remain here, whether thou wilt or no.
I am a spirit of no common rate:
The summer still doth tend upon my state;
And I do love thee: therefore go with me;
I'll give thee fairies to attend on thee;
And they shall fetch thee jewels from the deep,
And sing, while thou on pressed flowers dost sleep:
And I will purge thy mortal grossness so,
That thou shalt like an airy spirit go.
Peaseblossom! Cobweb! Moth! and Mustardseed!
   *Enter Four Fairies,* Peaseblossom, Cobweb,
    Moth, *and* Mustardseed

*First Fairy.* Ready.

*Second Fairy.*   And I.

*Third Fairy.*    And I.

*Fourth Fairy.*     And I.

*All.*       Where shall we go?

*Titania.* Be kind and courteous to this gentleman;
Hop in his walks, and gambol in his eyes;
Feed him with apricocks and dewberries,
With purple grapes, green figs, and mulberries;
The honey-bags steal from the humble-bees,
And for night-tapers crop their waxen thighs,
And light them at the fiery glow-worm's eyes,
To have my love to bed and to arise;
And pluck the wings from painted butterflies,

To fan the moonbeams from his sleeping eyes:
Nod to him, elves, and do him courtesies.

*First Fairy.* Hail, mortal!

*Second Fairy.* Hail!

*Third Fairy.* Hail!

*Fourth Fairy.* Hail!

*Bottom.* I cry your worship's mercy, heartily: I beseech your
worship's name?

*Cobweb.* Cobweb.

*Bottom.* I shall desire you of more acquaintance, good Master
Cobweb: if I cut my finger, I shall make bold with you. Your
name, honest gentleman?

*Peaseblossom.* Peaseblossom.

*Bottom.* I pray you, commend me to Mistress Squash, your
mother, and to Master Peascod, your father. Good Master
Peaseblossom, I shall desire you of more acquaintance too.
Your name, I beseech you, sir?

*Mustardseed.* Mustardseed.

*Bottom.* Good Master Mustardseed, I know your patience well:
that same cowardly, giant-like ox-beef hath devoured many a
gentleman of your house: I promise you, your kindred hath
made my eyes water ere now. I desire your more
acquaintance, good Master Mustardseed.

*Titania.* Come, wait upon him; lead him to my bower.
    The moon methinks looks with a watery eye;
And when she weeps, weeps every little flower,
    Lamenting some enforced chastity.
    Tie up my love's tongue, bring him silently.

                                                    *Exeunt.*

## scene 2.    [*Another part of the wood*]

*Enter* Oberon

*Oberon.* I wonder if Titania be awaked;
    Then, what it was that next came in her eye,
    Which she must dote on in extremity.
                *Enter* Puck
Here comes my messenger.
                      How now, mad spirit!
    What night-rule now about this haunted grove?

*Puck.* My mistress with a monster is in love.
    Near to her close and consecrated bower,
    While she was in her dull and sleeping hour,
    A crew of patches, rude mechanicals,
    That work for bread upon Athenian stalls,
    Were met together to rehearse a play
    Intended for great Theseus' nuptial-day.
    The shallowest thick-skin of that barren sort,
    Who Pyramus presented, in their sport
    Forsook his scene, and enter'd in a brake:
    When I did him at this advantage take,
    An ass's nole I fixed on his head:
    Anon his Thisbe must be answered,
    And forth my mimic comes. When they him spy,
    As wild geese that the creeping fowler eye,
    Or russet-pated choughs, many in sort,
    Rising and cawing at the gun's report,
    Sever themselves and madly sweep the sky,
    So, at his sight, away his fellows fly;
    And at our stamp, here o'er and o'er one falls;

He murder cries, and help from Athens calls.
Their sense thus weak, lost with their fears thus strong,
Made senseless things begin to do them wrong;
For briers and thorns at their apparel snatch;
Some sleeves, some hats, from yielders all things catch.
I led them on in this distracted fear,
And left sweet Pyramus translated there:
When in that moment, so it came to pass,
Titania waked, and straightway loved an ass.

*Oberon.* This falls out better than I could devise.
But hast thou yet latch'd the Athenian's eyes
With the love-juice, as I did bid thee do?

*Puck.* I took him sleeping—that is finish'd too—
And the Athenian woman by his side;
That when he waked, of force she must be eyed.

*Enter* Hermia *and* Demetrius

*Oberon.* Stand close: this is the same Athenian.

*Puck.* This is the woman, but not this the man.

*Demetrius.* O, why rebuke you him that loves you so?
Lay breath so bitter on your bitter foe.

*Hermia.* Now I but chide; but I should use thee worse,
For thou, I fear, hast given me cause to curse.
If thou hast slain Lysander in his sleep,
Being o'er shoes in blood, plunge in the deep,
And kill me too.
The sun was not so true unto the day
As he to me: would he have stol'n away
From sleeping Hermia? I'll believe as soon
This whole earth may be bored, and that the moon
May through the centre creep, and so displease
Her brother's noontide with th' Antipodes.

It cannot be but thou hast murder'd him;
So should a murderer look, so dead, so grim.

*Demetrius.* So should the murder'd look; and so should I,
Pierced through the heart with your stern cruelty:
Yet you, the murderer, look as bright, as clear,
As yonder Venus in her glimmering sphere.

*Hermia.* What's this to my Lysander? where is he?
Ah, good Demetrius, wilt thou give him me?

*Demetrius.* I had rather give his carcass to my hounds.

*Hermia.* Out, dog! out, cur! thou drivest me past the bounds
Of maiden's patience. Hast thou slain him, then?
Henceforth be never number'd among men!
O, once tell true, tell true, even for my sake!
Durst thou have look'd upon him being awake,
And hast thou kill'd him sleeping? O brave touch!
Could not a worm, an adder, do so much?
An adder did it; for with doubler tongue
Than thine, thou serpent, never adder stung.

*Demetrius.* You spend your passion on a misprised mood:
I am not guilty of Lysander's blood;
Nor is he dead, for aught that I can tell.

*Hermia.* I pray thee, tell me then that he is well.

*Demetrius.* An if I could, what should I get therefore?

*Hermia.* A privilege, never to see me more.
And from thy hated presence part I so:
See me no more, whether he be dead or no.

*Exit.*

*Demetrius.* There is no following her in this fierce vein:
Here therefore for a while I will remain.
So sorrow's heaviness doth heavier grow
For debt that bankrupt sleep doth sorrow owe;

Which now in some slight measure it will pay,
If for his tender here I make some stay.

*Lies down and sleeps.*

*Oberon.* What hast thou done? thou hast mistaken quite,
And laid the love-juice on some true-love's sight:
Of thy misprision must perforce ensue
Some true love turn'd, and not a false turn'd true.

*Puck.* Then fate o'er-rules, that, one man holding troth,
A million fail, confounding oath on oath.

*Oberon.* About the wood go swifter than the wind,
And Helena of Athens look thou find:
All fancy-sick she, is and pale of cheer
With sighs of love, that costs the fresh blood dear:
By some illusion see thou bring her here:
I'll charm his eyes against she do appear.

*Puck.* I go, I go; look how I go,
Swifter than arrow from the Tartar's bow.

*Exit.*

*Oberon.* [*Squeezing the juice on Demetrius's eyes.*]
Flower of this purple dye,
Hit with Cupid's archery,
Sink in apple of his eye.
When his love he doth espy,
Let her shine as gloriously
As the Venus of the sky.
When thou wakest, if she be by,
Beg of her for remedy.

*Re-enter* Puck

*Puck.* Captain of our fairy band,
Helena is here at hand;
And the youth, mistook by me,

Pleading for a lover's fee.
Shall we their fond pageant see?
Lord, what fools these mortals be!

*Oberon.* Stand aside: the noise they make
Will cause Demetrius to awake.

*Puck.* Then will two at once woo one;
That must needs be sport alone;
And those things do best please me
That befal preposterously.

Enter Lysander and Helena

*Lysander.* Why should you think that I should woo in scorn?
Scorn and derision never come in tears:
Look, when I vow, I weep; and vows so born,
In their nativity all truth appears.
How can these things in me seem scorn to you,
Bearing the badge of faith, to prove them true?

*Helena.* You do advance your cunning more and more.
When truth kills truth, O devilish-holy fray!
These vows are Hermia's: will you give her o'er?
Weigh oath with oath, and you will nothing weigh:
Your vows to her and me, put in two scales,
Will even weigh; and both as light as tales.

*Lysander.* I had no judgement when to her I swore.

*Helena.* Nor none, in my mind, now you give her o'er.

*Lysander.* Demetrius loves her, and he loves not you.

*Demetrius.* [*Awaking*] O Helen, goddess, nymph, perfect, divine!
To what, my love, shall I compare thine eyne?
Crystal is muddy. O, how ripe in show
Thy lips, those kissing cherries, tempting grow!
That pure congealed white, high Taurus' snow,
Fann'd with the eastern wind; turns to a crow

When thou hold'st up thy hand: O, let me kiss
This princess of pure white, this seal of bliss!

*Helena.* O spite! O hell! I see you all are bent
To set against me for your merriment:
If you were civil and knew courtesy,
You would not do me thus much injury.
Can you not hate me, as I know you do,
But you must join in souls to mock me too?
If you were men, as men you are in show,
You would not use a gentle lady so;
To vow, and swear, and superpraise my parts,
When I am sure you hate me with your hearts.
You both are rivals, and love Hermia;
And now both rivals, to mock Helena:
A trim exploit, a manly enterprise,
To conjure tears up in a poor maid's eyes
With your derision! none of noble sort
Would so offend a virgin, and extort
A poor soul's patience, all to make you sport.

*Lysander.* You are unkind, Demetrius; be not so;
For you love Hermia; this you know I know:
And here, with all good will, with all my heart,
In Hermia's love I yield you up my part;
And yours of Helena to me bequeath,
Whom I do love, and will do till my death.

*Helena.* Never did mockers waste more idle breath.

*Demetrius.* Lysander, keep thy Hermia; I will none:
If e'er I loved her, all that love is gone.
My heart to her but as guest-wise sojourn'd,
And now to Helen is it home return'd,
There to remain.

*Lysander.*          Helen, it is not so.

*Demetrius.* Disparage not the faith thou dost not know,
Lest, to thy peril, thou aby it dear.
Look, where thy love comes; yonder is thy dear.

*Re-enter* Hermia

*Hermia.* Dark night, that from the eye his function takes,
The ear more quick of apprehension makes;
Wherein it doth impair the seeing sense,
It pays the hearing double recompence.
Thou art not by mine eye, Lysander, found;
Mine ear, I thank it, brought me to thy sound.
But why unkindly didst thou leave me so?

*Lysander.* Why should he stay, whom love doth press to go?

*Hermia.* What love could press Lysander from my side?

*Lysander.* Lysander's love, that would not let him bide,
Fair Helena, who more engilds the night
Than all yon fiery oes and eyes of light.
Why seek'st thou me? could not this make thee know
The hate I bare thee made me leave thee so?

*Hermia.* You speak not as you think: it cannot be.

*Helena.* Lo, she is one of this confederacy!
Now I perceive they have conjoin'd all three
To fashion this false sport, in spite of me.
Injurious Hermia! most ungrateful maid!
Have you conspired, have you with these contrived
To bait me with this foul derision?
Is all the counsel that we two have shared,
The sisters' vows, the hours that we have spent
When we have chid the hasty-footed time
For parting us—O, is all forgot?
All school-days' friendship, childhood innocence?
We, Hermia, like two artificial gods,

Have with our needles created both one flower,
Both on one sampler, sitting on one cushion,
Both warbling of one song, both in one key;
As if our hands, our sides, voices, and minds,
Had been incorporate. So we grew together,
Like to a double cherry, seeming parted,
But yet an union in partition;
Two lovely berries moulded on one stem;
So, with two seeming bodies, but one heart;
Two of the first, like coats in heraldry,
Due but to one, and crowned with one crest.
And will you rent our ancient love asunder
To join with men in scorning your poor friend?
It is not friendly, 'tis not maidenly:
Our sex, as well as I, may chide you for it,
Though I alone do feel the injury.

*Hermia.* I am amazed at your passionate words.
I scorn you not: it seems that you scorn me.

*Helena.* Have you not set Lysander, as in scorn,
To follow me and praise my eyes and face?
And made your other love, Demetrius,
Who even but now did spurn me with his foot,
To call me goddess, nymph, divine and rare,
Precious, celestial? Wherefore speaks he this
To her he hates? and wherefore doth Lysander
Deny your love, so rich within his soul,
And tender me, forsooth, affection,
But by your setting on, by your consent?
What though I be not so in grace as you,
So hung upon with love, so fortunate,
But miserable most, to love unloved?
This you should pity rather than despise.

*Hermia.* I understand not what you mean by this.

*Helena.* Ay, do, persever, counterfeit sad looks,
Make mouths upon me when I turn my back;
Wink each at other; hold the sweet jest up:
This sport, well carried, shall be chronicled.
If you have any pity, grace, or manners,
You would not make me such an argument.
But fare ye well: 'tis partly my own fault,
Which death or absence soon shall remedy.

*Lysander.* Stay, gentle Helena; hear my excuse:
My love, my life, my soul, fair Helena!

*Helena.* O excellent!

*Hermia.* Sweet, do not scorn her so.

*Demetrius.* If she cannot entreat, I can compel.

*Lysander.* Thou canst compel no more than she entreat:
Thy threats have no more strength than her weak prayers.
Helen, I love thee; by my life, I do:
I swear by that which I will lose for thee,
To prove him false that says I love thee not.

*Demetrius.* I say I love thee more than he can do.

*Lysander.* If thou say so, withdraw, and prove it too.

*Demetrius.* Quick, come!

*Hermia.* Lysander, whereto tends all this?

*Lysander.* Away, you Ethiope!

*Demetrius.* No, no; he'll . . .
Seem to break loose. Take on as you would follow,
But yet come not: you are a tame man, go!

*Lysander.* Hang off, thou cat, thou burr! vile thing, let loose,
Or I will shake thee from me like a serpent!

*Hermia.* Why are you grown so rude? what change is this?
  Sweet love—

*Lysander.*       Thy love! out, tawny Tartar, out!
  Out, loathed medicine! hated potion, hence!

*Hermia.* Do you not jest?

*Helena.*             Yes, sooth; and so do you.

*Lysander.* Demetrius, I will keep my word with thee.

*Demetrius.* I would I had your bond, for I perceive
  A weak bond holds you: I'll not trust your word.

*Lysander.* What, should I hurt her, strike her, kill her dead?
  Although I hate her, I'll not harm her so.

*Hermia.* What, can you do me greater harm than hate?
  Hate me! wherefore? O me! what news, my love!
  Am not I Hermia? are not you Lysander?
  I am as fair now as I was erewhile.
  Since night you loved me; yet since night you left me:
  Why, then you left me—O, the gods forbid!—
  In earnest, shall I say?

*Lysander.*          Ay, by my life;
  And never did desire to see thee more.
  Therefore be out of hope, of question, of doubt;
  Be certain, nothing truer; 'tis no jest
  That I do hate thee, and love Helena.

*Hermia.* O me! [*To Helena*] you juggler! you canker-blossom!
  You thief of love! what, have you come by night
  And stolen my love's heart from him?

*Helena.*                      Fine, i'faith!
  Have you no modesty, no maiden shame,
  No touch of bashfulness? What, will you tear
  Impatient answers from my gentle tongue?
  Fie, fie! you counterfeit, you puppet, you!

*Hermia.* Puppet? why, so? ay, that way goes the game.
Now I perceive that she hath made compare
Between our statures; she hath urged her height;
And with her personage, her tall personage,
Her height, forsooth, she hath prevail'd with him.
And are you grown so high in his esteem,
Because I am so dwarfish and so low?
How low am I, thou painted maypole? speak;
How low am I? I am not yet so low
But that my nails can reach unto thine eyes.

*Helena.* I pray you, though you mock me, gentlemen,
Let her not hurt me: I was never curst;
I have no gift at all in shrewishness;
I am a right maid for my cowardice:
Let her not strike me. You perhaps may think,
Because she is something lower than myself,
That I can match her.

*Hermia.*                     Lower! hark, again.

*Helena.* Good Hermia, do not be so bitter with me.
I ever more did love you, Hermia,
Did ever keep your counsels, never wrong'd you;
Save that, in love unto Demetrius,
I told him of your stealth unto this wood.
He follow'd you; for love I follow'd him;
But he hath chid me hence, and threaten'd me
To strike me, spurn me, nay, to kill me too:
And now, so you will let me quiet go,
To Athens will I bear my folly back,
And follow you no further. Let me go:
You see how simple and how fond I am.

*Hermia.* Why, get you gone: who is't that hinders you?

*Helena.* A foolish heart, that I leave here behind.

*Hermia.* What, with Lysander?

*Helena.*                         With Demetrius.

*Lysander.* Be not afraid; she shall not harm thee, Helena.

*Demetrius.* No, sir, she shall not, though you take her part.

*Helena.* O, when she's angry, she is keen and shrewd!
　　She was a vixen when she went to school,
　　And though she be but little, she is fierce.

*Hermia.* Little again! nothing but 'low' and 'little'!
　　Why will you suffer her to flout me thus?
　　Let me come to her!

*Lysander.*                         Get you gone, you dwarf;
　　You minimus, of hindering knot-grass made;
　　You bead, you acorn.

*Demetrius.*                         You are too officious
　　In her behalf that scorns your services.
　　Let her alone: speak not of Helena;
　　Take not her part; for, if thou dost intend
　　Never so little show of love to her,
　　Thou shalt aby it.

*Lysander.*                         Now she holds me not;
　　Now follow, if thou darest, to try whose right,
　　Of thine or mine, is most in Helena.

*Demetrius.* Follow! nay, I'll go with thee, cheek by jole.

　　　　　　　　　*Exeunt* Lysander *and* Demetrius.

*Hermia.* You, mistress, all this coil is 'long of you:
　　Nay, go not back.

*Helena.*                         I will not trust you, I,
　　Nor longer stay in your curst company.
　　Your hands than mine are quicker for a fray,
　　My legs are longer though, to run away.

　　　　　　　　　　　　　*Exit.*

*Hermia.* I am amazed, and know not what to say.

*Exit.*

*Oberon.* This is thy negligence: still thou mistak'st,
  Or else committ'st thy knaveries wilfully.

*Puck.* Believe me, king of shadows, I mistook.
  Did not you tell me I should know the man
  By the Athenian garments he had on?
  And so far blameless proves my enterprise,
  That I have 'nointed an Athenian's eyes;
  And so far am I glad it so did sort,
  As this their jangling I esteem a sport.

*Oberon.* Thou see'st these lovers seek a place to fight:
  Hie therefore, Robin, overcast the night;
  The starry welkin cover thou anon
  With drooping fog, as black as Acheron;
  And lead these testy rivals so astray,
  As one come not within another's way.
  Like to Lysander sometime frame thy tongue,
  Then stir Demetrius up with bitter wrong;
  And sometime rail thou like Demetrius;
  And from each other look thou lead them thus,
  Till o'er their brows death-counterfeiting sleep
  With leaden legs and batty wings doth creep:
  Then crush this herb into Lysander's eye;
  Whose liquor hath this virtuous property,
  To take from thence all error with his might,
  And make his eyeballs roll with wonted sight.
  When they next awake, all this derision
  Shall seem a dream and fruitless vision;
  And back to Athens shall the lovers wend,
  With league whose date till death shall never end.
  Whiles I in this affair do thee employ,

I'll to my queen and beg her Indian boy;
And then I will her charmed eye release
From monster's view, and all things shall be peace.

*Puck.* My fairy lord, this must be done with haste,
For night's swift dragons cut the clouds full fast,
And yonder shines Aurora's harbinger;
At whose approach, ghosts wandering here and there
Troop home to churchyards: damned spirits all,
That in crossways and floods have burial,
Already to their wormy beds are gone;
For fear lest day should look their shames upon,
They wilfully themselves exile from light,
And must for aye consort with black-brow'd night.

*Oberon.* But we are spirits of another sort:
I with the morning's love have oft made sport;
And like a forester the groves may tread,
Even till the eastern gate, all fiery-red,
Opening on Neptune with fair blessed beams,
Turns into yellow gold his salt green streams.
But notwithstanding, haste; make no delay:
We may effect this business yet ere day.

*Exit.*

*Puck.* Up and down, up and down,
I will lead them up and down:
I am fear'd in field and town:
Goblin, lead them up and down.
Here comes one.

*Re-enter* Lysander

*Lysander.* Where art thou, proud Demetrius? speak thou now.

*Puck.* Here, villain; drawn and ready. Where art thou?

*Lysander.* I will be with thee straight.

*Puck.*                                    Follow me, then,
   To plainer ground.

                                *Exit* Lysander, *as following the voice.*

                  *Re-enter* Demetrius

*Demetrius.*                    Lysander! speak again:
   Thou runaway, thou coward, art thou fled?
   Speak! In some bush? Where dost thou hide thy head?

*Puck.* Thou coward, art thou bragging to the stars,
   Telling the bushes that thou look'st for wars,
   And wilt not come? Come, recreant; come, thou child;
   I'll whip thee with a rod: he is defiled
   That draws a sword on thee.

*Demetrius.*                    Yea, art thou there?

*Puck.* Follow my voice: we'll try no manhood here.

                                      *Exeunt.*

                  *Re-enter* Lysander

*Lysander.* He goes before me and still dares me on:
   When I come where he calls, then he is gone.
   The villain is much lighter-heel'd than I:
   I follow'd fast, but faster he did fly;
   That fallen am I in dark uneven way,
   And here will rest me. [*Lies down*] Come, thou gentle day!
   For if but once thou show me thy grey light,
   I'll find Demetrius, and revenge this spite.

                                      *Sleeps.*

                *Re-enter* Puck *and* Demetrius

*Puck.* Ho, ho, ho! Coward, why comest thou not?

*Demetrius.* Abide me, if thou darest; for well I wot
   Thou runn'st before me, shifting every place,
   And darest not stand, nor look me in the face
   Where art thou now?

*Puck.*                    Come hither: I am here.

*Demetrius.* Nay, then, thou mock'st me. Thou shalt buy this dear,
  If ever I thy face by daylight see:
  Now go thy way. Faintness constraineth me
  To measure out my length on this cold bed.
  By day's approach look to be visited.

*Lies down and sleeps.*

*Re-enter* Helena

*Helena.* O weary night, O long and tedious night,
    Abate thy hours! Shine comforts from the east,
  That I may back to Athens by daylight,
    From these that my poor company detest:
  And sleep, that sometimes shuts up sorrow's eye,
  Steal me awhile from mine own company.

*Lies down and sleeps.*

*Puck.* Yet but three? Come one more;
  Two of both kinds makes up four.
  Here she comes, curst and sad:
  Cupid is a knavish lad,
  Thus to make poor females mad.

*Re-enter* Hermia

*Hermia.* Never so weary, never so in woe;
    Bedabbled with the dew, and torn with briers;
  I can no further crawl, no further go;
    My legs can keep no pace with my desires.
  Here will I rest me till the break of day.
  Heavens shield Lysander, if they mean a fray!

*Lies down and sleeps.*

*Puck.*    On the ground
    Sleep sound:
    I'll apply

To your eye,
Gentle lover, remedy.

*Squeezing the juice on* Lysander's *eye.*

When thou wak'st,
Thou tak'st
True delight
In the sight
Of thy former lady's eye:
And the country proverb known,
That every man should take his own,
In your waking shall be shown:
Jack shall have Jill;
Nought shall go ill;
The man shall have his mare again, and all shall be well.

*Exit.*

# act 4

**scene 1.**   [*The same.* Lysander, Demetrius, Helena,
and Hermia, *lying asleep*]

*Enter* Titania *and* Bottom; Peaseblossom, Cobweb, Moth,
Mustardseed, *and other* Fairies *attending;* Oberon *behind unseen*

*Titania.* Come, sit thee down upon this flowery bed,
    While I thy amiable cheeks do coy,
And stick musk-roses in thy sleek smooth head,
    And kiss thy fair large ears, my gentle joy.

*Bottom.* Where's Peaseblossom?

*Peaseblossom.* Ready.

*Bottom.* Scratch my head, Peaseblossom. Where's Mounsieur
    Cobweb?

*Cobweb.* Ready.

*Bottom.* Mounsieur, Cobweb, good mounsieur, get you your
    weapons in your hand, and kill me a red-hipped humble-bee
    on the top of a thistle; and, good mounsieur, bring me the
    honey-bag. Do not fret yourself too much in the action,
    mounsieur; and good mounsieur, have a care the honey-bag

break not; I would be loth to have you overflown with a honey-bag, signior. Where's Mounsieur Mustardseed?

*Mustardseed.* Ready.

*Bottom.* Give me your neaf, Mounsieur Mustardseed. Pray you, leave your courtesy, good mounsieur.

*Mustardseed.* What's your will?

*Bottom.* Nothing, good mounsieur, but to help Cavalery Cobweb to scratch. I must to the barber's, mounsieur; for methinks I am marvellous hairy about the face; and I am such a tender ass, if my hair do but tickle me, I must scratch.

*Titania.* What, wilt thou hear some music, my sweet love?

*Bottom.* I have a reasonable good ear in music. Let's have the tongs and the bones.

*Titania.* Or say, sweet love, what thou desir'st to eat?

*Bottom.* Truly, a peck of provender: I could munch your good dry oats. Methinks I have a great desire to a bottle of hay: good hay, sweet hay, hath no fellow.

*Titania.* I have a venturous fairy that shall seek
The squirrel's hoard, and fetch thee new nuts.

*Bottom.* I had rather have a handful or two of dried peas.
But, I pray you, let none of your people stir me: I have an exposition of sleep come upon me.

*Titania.* Sleep thou, and I will wind thee in my arms.
Fairies, be gone, and be all ways away.

*Exeunt* Fairies.

So doth the woodbine the sweet honeysuckle
Gently entwist; the female ivy so
Enrings the barky fingers of the elm.
O, how I love thee! how I dote on thee!

*They sleep.*

*Enter* Puck

*Oberon.* [*Advancing*] Welcome, good Robin. See'st thou this
   sweet sight?
   Her dotage now I do begin to pity:
   For, meeting her of late behind the wood,
   Seeking sweet favours for this hateful fool,
   I did upbraid her and fall out with her;
   For she his hairy temples then had rounded
   With coronet of fresh and fragrant flowers;
   And that some dew, which sometime on the buds
   Was wont to swell like round and orient pearls,
   Stood now within the pretty flowerets' eyes,
   Like tears, that did their own disgrace bewail.
   When I had at my pleasure taunted her,
   And she in mild terms begg'd my patience,
   I then did ask of her her changeling child;
   Which straight she gave me, and her fairy sent
   To bear him to my bower in fairy land.
   And now I have the boy, I will undo
   This hateful imperfection of her eyes:
   And, gentle Puck, take this transformed scalp
   From off the head of this Athenian swain;
   That, he awaking when the other do,
   May all to Athens back again repair,
   And think no more of this night's accidents,
   But as the fierce vexation of a dream.
   But first I will release the fairy queen.

                      *Squeezes the juice on Titania's eyes.*

     Be as thou wast wont to be;
     See as thou wast wont to see:
     Dian's bud o'er Cupid's flower
     Hath such force and blessed power.
    Now, my Titania; wake you, my sweet queen.

*Titania.* My Oberon! what visions have I seen!
  Methought I was enamour'd of an ass.

*Oberon.* There lies your love.

*Titania.*                    How came these things to pass?
  O, how mine eyes do loathe his visage now!

*Oberon.* Silence awhile. Robin, take off this head.
  Titania, music call; and strike more dead
  Than common sleep of all these five the sense.

*Titania.* Music, ho! music, such as charmeth sleep!

                                        *Music, still.*

*Puck.* Now, when thou wak'st, with thine own fool's eyes peep.

*Oberon.* Sound, music! Come, my queen, take hands with me,
  And rock the ground whereon these sleepers be.
  Now thou and I are new in amity,
  And will to-morrow midnight solemnly
  Dance in Duke Theseus' house triumphantly,
  And bless it to all fair prosperity:
  There shall the pairs of faithful lovers be
  Wedded, with Theseus, all in jollity.

*Puck.* Fairy king, attend, and mark:
  I do hear the morning lark.

*Oberon.* Then, my queen, in silence sad,
  Trip we after night's shade:
  We the globe can compáss soon,
  Swifter than the wandering moon.

*Titania.* Come, my lord; and in our flight,
  Tell me how it came this night,
  That I sleeping here was found
  With these mortals on the ground.

                                        *Exeunt.*
                                *Horns winded within.*

*Enter* Theseus, Hippolyta, Egeus, *and train*

*Theseus.* Go, one of you, find out the forester;
    For now our observation is perform'd;
    And since we have the vaward of the day,
    My love shall hear the music of my hounds.
    Uncouple in the western valley; let them go:
    Dispatch, I say, and find the forester.

                          *Exit an* Attendant.
    We will, fair queen, up to the mountain's top,
    And mark the musical confusion
    Of hounds and echo in conjunction.

*Hippolyta.* I was with Hercules and Cadmus once,
    When in a wood of Crete they bay'd the bear
    With hounds of Sparta: never did I hear
    Such gallant chiding; for, besides the groves,
    The skies, the fountains, every region near
    Seem'd all one mutual cry: I never heard
    So musical a discord, such sweet thunder.

*Theseus.* My hounds are bred out of the Spartan kind,
    So flew'd, so sanded; and their heads are hung
    With ears that sweep away the morning dew;
    Crook-knee'd, and dew-lapp'd like Thessalian bulls;
    Slow in pursuit, but match'd in mouth like bells,
    Each under each. A cry more tuneable
    Was never holla'd to, nor cheer'd with horn,
    In Crete, in Sparta, nor in Thessaly:
    Judge when you hear. But, soft! what nymphs are these?

*Egeus.* My lord, this is my daughter here asleep;
    And this, Lysander; this Demetrius is;
    This Helena, old Nedar's Helena:
    I wonder of their being here together.

*Theseus.* No doubt they rose up early to observe

The rite of May; and, hearing our intent,
Came here in grace of our solemnity.
But speak, Egeus; is not this the day
That Hermia should give answer of her choice?

*Egeus.* It is, my lord.

*Theseus.* Go, bid the huntsmen wake them with their horns.

> *Horns and shout within.* Lysander, Demetrius,
> Helena, *and* Hermia, *wake and start up.*

Good morrow, friends. Saint Valentine is past:
Begin these wood-birds but to couple now?

*Lysander.* Pardon, my lord.

*Theseus.*            I pray you all, stand up.
I know you two are rival enemies:
How comes this gentle concord in the world,
That hatred is so far from jealousy
To sleep by hate, and fear no enmity?

*Lysander.* My lord, I shall reply amazedly,
Half sleep, half walking: but as yet, I swear,
I cannot truly say how I came here;
But, as I think—for truly would I speak,
And now I do bethink me, so it is—
I came with Hermia hither: our intent
Was to be gone from Athens, where we might,
Without the peril of the Athenian law—

*Egeus.* Enough, enough, my lord; you have enough:
I beg the law, the law upon his head!
They would have stol'n away; they would, Demetrius,
Thereby to have defeated you and me,
You of your wife and me of my consent,
Of my consent that she should be your wife.

*Demetrius.* My lord, fair Helen told me of their stealth,

Of this their purpose hither to this wood;
And I in fury hither follow'd them,
Fair Helena in fancy following me.
But, my good lord, I wot not by what power—
But by some power it is—my love to Hermia,
Melted as the snow, seems to me now
As the remembrance of an idle gaud,
Which in my childhood I did dote upon;
And all the faith, the virtue of my heart,
The object and the pleasure of mine eye,
Is only Helena. To her, my lord,
Was I betroth'd ere I saw Hermia:
But like in sickness did I loathe this food;
But as in health, come to my natural taste,
Now I do wish it, love it, long for it,
And will for evermore be true to it.

*Theseus.* Fair lovers, you are fortunately met:
Of this discourse we more will hear anon.
Egeus, I will overbear your will;
For in the temple, by and by, with us
These couples shall eternally be knit:
And, for the morning now is something worn,
Our purposed hunting shall be set aside.
Away with us to Athens! three and three,
We'll hold a feast in great solemnity.
Come, Hippolyta.

                    *Exeunt* Theseus, Hippolyta, Egeus, *and train*.

*Demetrius.* These things seem small and undistinguishable,
Like far-off mountains turned into clouds.

*Hermia.* Methinks I see these things with parted eye,
When everything seems double.

*Helena.*                              So methinks:

And I have found Demetrius like a jewel,
Mine own, and not mine own.

*Demetrius.*                               Are you sure
  That we are awake? It seems to me
  That yet we sleep, we dream. Do not you think
  The Duke was here, and bid us follow him?

*Hermia.* Yea, and my father.

*Helena.*                          And Hippolyta.

*Lysander.* And he did bid us follow to the temple.

*Demetrius.* Why, then, we are awake: let's follow him;
  And by the way let us recount our dreams.

*Exeunt.*

*Bottom.* [*Awaking*] When my cue comes, call me, and I will
  answer: my next is, 'Most fair Pyramus.' Heigh-ho! Peter
  Quince! Flute, the bellows-mender! Snout, the tinker!
  Starveling! God's my life, stolen hence, and left me asleep! I
  have had a most rare vision. I have had a dream, past the wit
  of man to say what dream it was: man is but an ass, if he go
  about to expound this dream. Methought I was—there is no
  man can tell what. Methought I was—and methought I
  had—but man is but a patched fool if he will offer to say
  what methought I had. The eye of man hath not heard, the
  ear of man hath not seen, man's hand is not able to taste, his
  tongue to conceive, nor his heart to report, what my dream
  was. I will get Peter Quince to write a ballad of this dream:
  it shall be called Bottom's Dream, because it hath no bottom;
  and I will sing it in the latter end of a play, before the Duke:
  peradventure, to make it the more gracious, I shall sing it at
  her death.

*Exit.*

## scene 2.  [*Athens.* Quince's *house*]

*Enter* Quince, Flute, Snout, *and* Starveling

*Quince.* Have you sent to Bottom's house? is he come home yet?

*Starveling.* He cannot be heard of. Out of doubt he is
transported.

*Flute.* If he come not, then the play is marred: it goes not
forward, doth it?

*Quince.* It is not possible: you have not a man in all Athens able
to discharge Pyramus but he.

*Flute.* No, he hath simply the best wit of any handicraft man in
Athens.

*Quince.* Yea, and the best person too; and he is a very paramour
for a sweet voice.

*Flute.* You must say 'paragon': a paramour is, God bless us, a
thing of naught.

*Enter* Snug

*Snug.* Masters, the Duke is coming from the temple, and there is
two or three lords and ladies more married: if our sport had
gone forward, we had all been made men.

*Flute.* O sweet bully Bottom! Thus hath he lost sixpence a day
during his life; he could not have 'scaped sixpence a day: an
the Duke had not given him sixpence a day for playing
Pyramus, I'll be hanged; he would have deserved it: sixpence
a day in Pyramus, or nothing.

*Enter* Bottom

*Bottom.* Where are these lads? where are these hearts?

*Quince.* Bottom! O most courageous day! O most happy hour!

*Bottom.* Masters, I am to discourse wonders: but ask me not what; for if I tell you, I am no true Athenian. I will tell you everything, right as it fell out.

*Quince.* Let us hear, sweet Bottom.

*Bottom.* Not a word of me. All that I will tell you is, that the Duke hath dined. Get your apparel together, good strings to your beards, new ribbons to your pumps; meet presently at the palace; every man look o'er his part; for the short and the long is, our play is preferred. In any case, let Thisby have clean linen; and let not him that plays the lion pare his nails, for they shall hang out for the lion's claws. And, most dear actors, eat no onions nor garlic, for we are to utter sweet breath; and I do not doubt but to hear them say, it is a sweet comedy. No more words: away! go, away!

*Exeunt.*

# act 5

**scene 1.** [*Athens. The palace of* Theseus]

*Enter* Theseus, Hippolyta, Philostrate, Lords,
*and* Attendants

*Hippolyta.* 'Tis strange, my Theseus, that these lovers speak of.

*Theseus.* More strange than true: I never may believe
  These antique fables, nor these fairy toys.
  Lovers and madmen have such seething brains,
  Such shaping fantasies, that apprehend
  More than cool reason ever comprehends.
  The lunatic, the lover, and the poet
  Are of imagination all compact:
  One sees more devils than vast hell can hold,
  That is the madman: the lover, all as frantic,
  Sees Helen's beauty in a brow of Egypt:
  The poet's eye, in a fine frenzy rolling,
  Doth glance from heaven to earth, from earth to heaven;
  And as imagination bodies forth
  The forms of things unknown, the poet's pen
  Turns them to shapes, and gives to airy nothing

A local habitation and a name.
Such tricks hath strong imagination,
That if it would but apprehend some joy,
It comprehends some bringer of that joy;
Or in the night, imagining some fear,
How easy is a bush supposed a bear!

*Hippolyta.* But all the story of the night told over,
And all their minds transfigured so together,
More witnesseth than fancy's images,
And grows to something of great constancy;
But, howsoever, strange and admirable.

*Theseus.* Here come the lovers, full of joy and mirth.
            *Enter* Lysander, Demetrius, Hermia, *and* Helena
Joy, gentle friends! joy and fresh days of love
Accompany your hearts!

*Lysander.*                More than to us
Wait in your royal walks, your board, your bed!

*Theseus.* Come now; what masques, what dances shall we have,
To wear away this long age of three hours
Between our after-supper and bed-time?
Where is our usual manager of mirth?
What revels are in hand? Is there no play
To ease the anguish of a torturing hour?
Call Philostrate.

*Philostrate.*        Here, mighty Theseus.

*Theseus.* Say, what abridgement have you for this evening?
What masque? what music? How shall we beguile
The lazy time, if not with some delight?

*Philostrate.* There is a brief how many sports are ripe:
Make choice of which your highness will see first.
                                        *Giving a paper.*

*Theseus.* [*Reads*]   The battle with the Centaurs, to be sung
                         By an Athenian eunuch to the harp.

We'll none of that: that have I told my love,
In glory of my kinsman Hercules.

[*Reads*]   The riot of the tipsy Bacchanals,
              Tearing the Thracian singer in their rage.

That is an old device; and it was play'd
When I from Thebes came last a conqueror.

[*Reads*]   The thrice three Muses mourning for the death
              Of Learning, late deceased in beggary.

That is some satire, keen and critical,
Not sorting with a nuptial ceremony.

[*Reads*]   A tedious brief scene of young Pyramus
              And his love Thisbe; very tragical mirth.

Merry and tragical! tedious and brief!
That is, hot ice and wondrous strange snow.
How shall we find the concord of this discord?

*Philostrate.* A play there is, my lord, some ten words long,
   Which is as brief as I have known a play;
   But by ten words, my lord, it is too long,
   Which makes it tedious; for in all the play
   There is not one word apt, one player fitted:
   And tragical, my noble lord, it is;
   For Pyramus therein doth kill himself.
   Which, when I saw rehearsed, I must confess,
   Made mine eyes water; but more merry tears
   The passion of loud laughter never shed.

*Theseus.* What are they that do play it?

*Philostrate.* Hard-handed men, that work in Athens here,
   Which never labour'd in their minds till now;
   And now have toil'd their unbreathed memories
   With this same play, against your nuptial.

*Theseus.* And we will hear it.

*Philostrate.*                    No, my noble lord;
    It is not for you: I have heard it over,
    And it is nothing, nothing in the world;
    Unless you can find sport in their intents,
    Extremely stretch'd and conn'd with cruel pain
    To do you service.

*Theseus.*                    I will hear that play;
    For never anything can be amiss,
    When simpleness and duty tender it.
    Go, bring them in: and take your places, ladies.

                        *Exit* Philostrate.

*Hippolyta.* I love not to see wretchedness o'ercharged,
    And duty in his service perishing.

*Theseus.* Why, gentle sweet, you shall see no such thing.

*Hippolyta.* He says they can do nothing in this kind.

*Theseus.* The kinder we, to give them thanks for nothing.
    Our sport shall be to take what they mistake:
    And what poor duty cannot do, noble respect
    Takes it in might, not merit.
    Where I have come, great clerks have purposed
    To greet me with premeditated welcomes;
    Where I have seen them shiver and look pale,
    Make periods in the midst of sentences,
    Throttle their practised accent in their fears,
    And, in conclusion, dumbly have broke off,
    Not paying me a welcome. Trust me, sweet,
    Out of this silence yet I picked a welcome;
    And in the modesty of fearful duty
    I read as much as from the rattling tongue
    Of saucy and audacious eloquence.

Love, therefore, and tongue-tied simplicity
In least speak most, to my capacity.

*Re-enter* Philostrate

*Philostrate.* So please your Grace, the Prologue is address'd.

*Theseus.* Let him approach.

*Flourish of trumpets.*

*Enter* Quince *for the* Prologue

*Prologue.*      If we offend, it is with our good will.
            That you should think, we come not to offend,
    But with good will. To show our simple skill,
            That is the true beginning of our end.
    Consider, then, we come but in despite.
            We do not come, as minding to content you,
    Our true intent is. All for your delight,
            We are not here. That you should here repent you,
    The actors are at hand; and, by their show,
    You shall know all, that you are like to know.

*Theseus.* This fellow doth not stand upon points.

*Lysander.* He hath rid his prologue like a rough colt; he knows
not the stop. A good moral, my lord: it is not enough to
speak, but to speak true.

*Hippolyta.* Indeed he hath played on his prologue like a child on
a recorder; a sound, but not in government.

*Theseus.* His speech was like a tangled chain; nothing impaired,
but all disordered. Who is next?

*Enter* Pyramus *and* Thisbe, Wall, Moonshine, *and* Lion

*Prologue.*   Gentles, perchance you wonder at this show;
            But wonder on, till truth make all things plain.
    This man is Pyramus, if you would know;
            This beauteous lady Thisby is certain.
    This man, with lime and rough-cast, doth present
            Wall, that vile Wall which did these lovers sunder;
    And through Wall's chink, poor souls, they are content

To whisper. At the which let no man wonder.
This man, with lanthorn, dog, and bush of thorn,
Presenteth Moonshine; for, if you will know,
By moonshine did these lovers think no scorn
To meet at Ninus' tomb, there, there to woo.
This grisly beast, which Lion hight by name,
The trusty Thisby, coming first by night,
Did scare away, or rather did affright;
And, as she fled, her mantle she did fall,
Which Lion vile with bloody mouth did stain.
Anon comes Pyramus, sweet youth and tall,
And finds his trusty Thisby's mantle slain:
Whereat, with blade, with bloody blameful blade,
He bravely broach'd his boiling bloody breast;
And Thisby, tarrying in mulberry shade,
His dagger drew, and died. For all the rest,
Let Lion, Moonshine, Wall, and lovers twain
At large discourse, while here they do remain.

*Exeunt* Prologue, Pyramus, Thisbe, Lion *and* Moonshine.

*Theseus.* I wonder if the lion be to speak.

*Demetrius.* No wonder, my lord: one lion may, when many asses do.

*Wall.*   In this same interlude it doth befall
That I, one Snout by name, present a wall;
And such a wall, as I would have you think,
That had in it a crannied hole or chink,
Through which the lovers, Pyramus and Thisby,
Did whisper often very secretly.
This loam, this rough-cast, and this stone doth show
That I am that same wall; the truth is so:
And this the cranny is, right and sinister,
Through which the fearful lovers are to whisper.

*Theseus.* Would you desire lime and hair to speak better?

*Demetrius.* It is the wittiest partition that ever I heard discourse, my lord.

*Theseus.* Pyramus draws near the wall: silence!

*Re-enter* Pyramus

*Pyramus.*    O grim-look'd night! O night with hue so black!
        O night, which ever art when day is not!
    O night, O night! alack, alack, alack,
        I fear my Thisby's promise is forgot!
    And thou, O wall, O sweet, O lovely wall,
        That stand'st between her father's ground and mine!
    Thou wall, O wall, O sweet and lovely wall,
        Show me thy chink, to blink through with mine eyne!

Wall *holds up his fingers.*

    Thanks, courteous wall: Jove shield thee well for this!
        But what see I? No Thisby do I see.
    O wicked wall, through whom I see no bliss!
        Cursed be thy stones for thus deceiving me!

*Theseus.* The wall, methinks, being sensible, should curse again.

*Pyramus.* No, in truth, sir, he should not. 'Deceiving me' is
    Thisby's cue: she is to enter now, and I am to spy her through
    the wall. You shall see, it will fall pat as I told you. Yonder
    she comes.

*Re-enter* Thisbe

*Thisbe.*    O wall, full often hast thou heard my moans,
        For parting my fair Pyramus and me!
    My cherry lips have often kiss'd thy stones,
        Thy stones with lime and hair knit up in thee.

*Pyramus.*    I see a voice: now will I to the chink,
        To spy an I can hear my Thisby's face.
    Thisby!

*Thisbe.*        My love thou art, my love I think.

*Pyramus.*        Think what thou wilt, I am thy lover's grace;
        And, like Limander, am I trusty still.

*Thisbe.*    And I like Helen, till the Fates me kill.

*Pyramus.*    Not Shafalus to Procrus was so true.

| | |
|---|---|
| *Thisbe.* | As Shafalus to Procrus, I to you. |
| *Pyramus.* | O, kiss me through the hole of this vile wall! |
| *Thisbe.* | I kiss the wall's hole, not your lips at all. |
| *Pyramus.* | Wilt thou at *Ninny*'s tomb meet me straightway? |
| *Thisbe.* | 'Tide life, 'tide death, I come without delay. |

> *Exeunt* Pyramus *and* Thisbe.

| | |
|---|---|
| *Wall.* | Thus have I, wall, my part discharged so; |
| | And, being done, thus wall away doth go. |

> *Exit.*

*Theseus.* Now is the mural down between the two neighbours.

*Demetrius.* No remedy, my lord, when walls are so wilful to hear without warning.

*Hippolyta.* This is the silliest stuff that ever I heard.

*Theseus.* The best in this kind are but shadows; and the worst are no worse, if imagination amend them.

*Hippolyta.* It must be your imagination then, and not theirs.

*Theseus.* If we imagine no worse of them than they of themselves, they may pass for excellent men. Here come two noble beasts in, a man and a lion.

*Re-enter* Lion *and* Moonshine

| | |
|---|---|
| *Lion.* | You ladies, you whose gentle hearts do fear |
| | The smallest monstrous mouse that creeps on floor, |
| | May now perchance both quake and tremble here, |
| | When lion rough in wildest rage doth roar. |
| | Then know that I, one Snug the joiner, am |
| | A lion-fell, nor else no lion's dam; |
| | For if I should as lion come in strife |
| | Into this place, 'twere pity on my life. |

*Theseus.* A very gentle beast, and of a good conscience.

*Demetrius.* The very best at a beast, my lord, that e'er I saw.

*Lysander.* This lion is a very fox for his valour.

*Theseus.* True; and a goose for his discretion.

*Demetrius.* Not so, my lord; for his valour cannot carry his discretion; and the fox carries the goose.

*Theseus.* His discretion, I am sure, cannot carry his valour; for the goose carries not the fox. It is well: leave it to his discretion, and let us listen to the moon.

*Moonshine.* This lanthorn doth the horned moon present—

*Demetrius.* He should have worn the horns on his head.

*Theseus.* He is no crescent, and his horns are invisible within the circumference.

*Moonshine.* This lanthorn doth the horned moon present;
Myself the Man i' the Moon do seem to be.

*Theseus.* This is the greatest error of all the rest: the man should be put into the lantern. How is it else the Man i' the Moon?

*Demetrius.* He dares not come there for the candle; for you see it is already in snuff.

*Hippolyta.* I am aweary of this moon: would he would change!

*Theseus.* It appears, by his small light of discretion, that he is in the wane; but yet in courtesy, in all reason, we must stay the time.

*Lysander.* Proceed, Moon.

*Moonshine.* All that I have to say, is, to tell you that the lanthorn is the moon; I, the Man i' the Moon; this thorn-bush, my thorn-bush; and this dog, my dog.

*Demetrius.* Why, all these should be in the lantern, for all these are in the moon. But, silence! here comes Thisbe.

*Re-enter* Thisbe

*Thisbe.* This is old Ninny's tomb. Where is my love?

*Lion.* [*Roaring*] Oh—!

Thisbe *runs off.*

*Demetrius.* Well roared, Lion.

*Theseus.* Well run, Thisbe.

*Hippolyta.* Well shone, Moon. Truly, the moon shines with a good grace.

> *The* Lion *shakes* Thisbe's *mantle, and exit.*

*Theseus.* Well moused, Lion.

*Demetrius.* And then came Pyramus.

*Lysander.* And so the lion vanished.

> *Re-enter* Pyramus

*Pyramus.*  Sweet Moon, I thank thee for thy sunny beams;
I thank thee, Moon, for shining now so bright;
For, by thy gracious, golden, glittering gleams,
    I trust to take of truest Thisby sight.
            But stay, O spite!
            But mark, poor knight,
    What dreadful dole is here!
            Eyes, do you see?
            How can it be?
    O dainty duck! O dear!
            Thy mantle good,
            What, stain'd with blood!
    Approach, ye Furies fell!
            O Fates, come, come,
            Cut thread and thrum;
    Quail, crush, conclude, and quell!

*Theseus.* This passion, and the death of a dear friend, would go near to make a man look sad.

*Hippolyta.* Beshrew my heart, but I pity the man.

*Pyramus.*  O wherefore, Nature, didst thou lions frame?
        Since lion vile hath here deflower'd my dear:
    Which is—no, no—which was the fairest dame
        That lived, that loved, that liked, that look'd with cheer.
            Come, tears, confound;
            Out, sword, and wound

The pap of Pyramus;
    Ay, that left pap,
    Where heart doth hop:

                                    *Stabs himself.*

Thus die I, thus, thus, thus.
    Now am I dead,
    Now am I fled;
My soul is in the sky:
    Tongue, lose thy light;
    Moon, take thy flight:

                                *Exit* Moonshine.
Now die, die, die, die, die.

                                        *Dies.*

*Demetrius.* No die, but an ace, for him; for he is but one.

*Lysander.* Less than an ace, man; for he is dead; he is nothing.

*Theseus.* With the help of a surgeon he might yet recover, and prove an ass.

*Hippolyta.* How chance Moonshine is gone before Thisbe comes back and finds her lover?

*Theseus.* She will find him by starlight. Here she comes, and her passion ends the play.

                    *Re-enter* Thisbe

*Hippolyta.* Methinks she should not use a long one for such a Pyramus: I hope she will be brief.

*Demetrius.* A mote will turn the balance, which Pyramus, which Thisbe, is the better; he for a man, God warrant us; she for a woman, God bless us.

*Lysander.* She hath spied him already with those sweet eyes.

*Demetrius.* And thus she means, videlicet:—

*Thisbe.*                 Asleep, my love?
                    What, dead, my dove?
                O Pyramus, arise!
                    Speak, speak. Quite dumb?
                    Dead, dead? A tomb

Must cover thy sweet eyes.
 These lily lips,
 This cherry nose,
These yellow cowslip cheeks,
 Are gone, are gone:
 Lovers, make moan:
His eyes were green as leeks.
 O Sisters Three,
 Come, come to me,
With hands as pale as milk;
 Lay them in gore,
 Since you have shore
With shears his thread of silk.
 Tongue, not a word:
 Come, trusty sword;
Come, blade, my breast imbrue:

            *Stabs herself.*

 And farewell, friends;
 Thus Thisby ends:
Adieu, adieu, adieu.

               *Dies.*

*Theseus.* Moonshine and Lion are left to bury the dead.

*Demetrius.* Ay, and Wall too.

*Bottom.* [*Starting up*] No, I assure you; the wall is down that parted their fathers. Will it please you to see the epilogue, or to hear a Bergomask dance between two of our company?

*Theseus.* No epilogue, I pray you; for your play needs no excuse. Never excuse; for when the players are all dead, there need none to be blamed. Marry, if he that writ it had played Pyramus and hanged himself in Thisbe's garter, it would have been a fine tragedy: and so it is, truly; and very notably discharged. But, come, your Bergomask: let your epilogue alone.

       *The* Mechanicals *dance, then exit.*

The iron tongue of midnight hath told twelve:
Lovers, to bed; 'tis almost fairy time.
I fear we shall out-sleep the coming morn,
As much as we this night have overwatch'd.
This palpable-gross play hath well beguiled
The heavy gait of night. Sweet friends, to bed.
A fortnight hold we this solemnity,
In nightly revels and new jollity.

*Exeunt.*

*Enter* Puck

*Puck.* Now the hungry lion roars,
    And the wolf behowls the moon;
Whilst the heavy ploughman snores,
    All with weary task fordone.
Now the wasted brands do glow,
    Whilst the screech-owl, screeching loud,
Puts the wretch that lies in woe
    In remembrance of a shroud.
Now it is the time of night
    That the graves, all gaping wide,
Every one lets forth his sprite
    In the church-way paths to glide:
And we fairies, that do run
    By the triple Hecate's team
From the presence of the sun,
    Following darkness like a dream,
Now are frolic: not a mouse
Shall disturb this hallow'd house:
I am sent with broom before
To sweep the dust behind the door.
            *Enter* Oberon *and* Titania *with their train*

*Oberon*. Through the house give glimmering light,
    By the dead and drowsy fire:
Every elf and fairy sprite
    Hop as light as bird from brier;
And this ditty, after me,
Sing, and dance it trippingly.

*Titania*. First, rehearse your song by rote,
    To each word a warbling note:
Hand in hand, with fairy grace,
Will we sing, and bless this place.

                                            *Song and dance.*

*Oberon*. Now, until the break of day,
Through this house each fairy stray.
To the best bride-bed will we,
Which by us shall blessed be;
And the issue there create
Ever shall be fortunate.
So shall all the couples three
Ever true in loving be;
And the blots of Nature's hand
Shall not in their issue stand;
Never mole, hare lip, nor scar,
Nor mark prodigious, such as are
Despised in nativity,
Shall upon their children be.
With this field-dew consecrate,
Every fairy take his gait;
And each several chamber bless,
Through this palace with sweet peace,
And the owner of it blest,
Ever shall in safety rest.
Trip away; make no stay;

Meet me all by break of day.

*Exeunt* Oberon, Titania, *and train.*

*Puck.* [*To the audience.*] If we shadows have offended,
Think but this, and all is mended,
That you have but slumber'd here,
While these visions did appear.
And this weak and idle theme,
No more yielding but a dream,

Gentles, do not reprehend:
If you pardon, we will mend.
And, as I am an honest Puck,
If we have unearned luck
Now to 'scape the serpent's tongue,
We will make amends ere long;
Else the Puck a liar call:
So, good night unto you all.
Give me your hands, if we be friends,
And Robin shall restore amends.

*Exit.*